Project Risk Governance

Project Risk Governance

Managing Uncertainty and Creating Organisational Value

DIETER FINK
School of Management at Edith Cowan University, Australia

Routledge
Taylor & Francis Group

LONDON AND NEW YORK

First published 2013 by Gower Publishing

2 Park Square, Milton Park, Abingdon, Oxon OX14 4RN
711 Third Avenue, New York, NY 10017, USA

Routledge is an imprint of the Taylor & Francis Group, an informa business

First issued in paperback 2016

Gower Applied Business Research
Our programme provides leaders, practitioners, scholars and researchers with thought provoking, cutting edge books that combine conceptual insights, interdisciplinary rigour and practical relevance in key areas of business and management.

British Library Cataloguing in Publication Data
A catalogue record for this book is available from the British Library

Library of Congress Cataloging-in-Publication Data
Fink, Dieter.
 Project risk governance : managing uncertainty and creating organizational value / by Dieter Fink.
    pages cm
 Includes bibliographical references and index.
 ISBN 978-1-4724-1904-0 (hardback)
 1. Project management. 2. Risk management. I. Title.
 HD69.P75F543 2013
 658.4'04--dc23

                                                                                    2013022019

ISBN 978-1-4724-1904-0 (hbk)
ISBN 978-1-138-26955-2 (pbk)

Contents

List of Figures

List of Tables

List of Abbreviations

ABR	Active Benefits Realisation
AIPM	Australian Institute of Project Managers
APM	Academy for Project Management
ASX	Australian Stock Exchange
BOK	Body of Knowledge
BSC	Balanced Scorecard
CBA	Cost–Benefit Analysis
CG	Corporate Governance
CMM	Capability Maturity Model
COSO	Committee of Sponsoring Organizations of the Treadway Commission
CPM	Corporate Performance Management
DCF	Discounted Cash Flow
ERM	Enterprise Risk Management
FMO	Functional Matrix Organisation
HRM	Human Resources Management
IRR	Internal Rate of Return
ISACA	Information Systems Audit and Control Association
ISO	International Organization for Standardization
IT	Information Technology
ITGI	Information Technology Governance Institute
KPA	Key Process Area
NPV	Net Present Value
OECD	Organisation for Economic Co-operation and Development
OPM3®	Organisational Project Management Maturity Model
P3M3®	Portfolio, Programme and Project Management Maturity Model
PBO	Project-Based Organisation
PEST	Political/Legal, Environmental, Socio-cultural and Technological analysis
PG	Project Governance

PMBOK®   Project Management Body of Knowledge
PMI   Project Management Institute
PMM   Project Management Maturity model
PMO   Project Management Office
PP   Payback Period
PPMO   Project Portfolio Management Office
PRG   Project Risk Governance
PRINCE2™   PRojects IN Controlled Environments
RBS   Risk Breakdown Structure
RM-CMM   Risk Management Capability Maturity Model
ROI   Return on Investment
SOE   Standard Operating Environment
SWOT   Strengths, Weaknesses, Opportunities and Threats analysis
WBS   Work Breakdown Structure

About the Author

Dieter Fink is an Associate Professor in the School of Management at Edith Cowan University in Perth, Western Australia. He previously worked as a Systems Engineer for IBM and as Manager, Information Technology Consulting, for Arthur Young (now Ernst & Young) for whom he carried out a number of project management assignments. He teaches a Master's-level course in project risk management in his university. In 2011, the Australian Institute of Project Management provided him with research support to identify from its membership the key issues in project risk management for the next three to five years. Over the past 20 years he has authored a book on security management and published over 70 refereed research papers in a wide range of international journals and conference proceedings.

Foreword

Our lives have become more complex as a multitude of situations demand our attention, virtually on a daily basis. We are confronted by numerous issues which are often complex and unrelated. Many choices present themselves but how we react must take into account the consequences of our actions. They have to be carefully evaluated in order to make decisions with our best interests in mind.

Risk plays a crucial role in our deliberations primarily because of the uncertainty of the outcomes of our actions. Most of us perceive the existence of risk as the precursor of negative outcomes, and therefore something to be avoided or at least mitigated as far as possible. Should the identified risk be considered too great, we are likely to act defensively, for example by rejecting a 'risky' proposition that has been put to us.

Yet without taking on risk we cannot prosper. Our way of life seeks to gain continuous improvement, and this is not possible without innovation and entrepreneurship. New developments, be they in technology, transportation, medicine or other endeavours, depend on our ability to 'risk' capital, time and effort in order to achieve a breakthrough. To avoid risk is to stifle our ability to realise the value of opportunities as they become apparent, despite the opportunity, at first glance, looking risky.

A shift in attitude is required to see both positive and negative outcomes in the presence of risk. While the latter has traditionally been the primary focus of risk management, the former is a strategy in which risk is perceived as a value-creating opportunity that can be exploited. In the past, the emphasis was on value-protecting through controlling the impact of negative risks, whereas now to take a risk is to gain advantage. Those organisations prepared to take on risks and applying sound risk management practices will prosper in an increasingly competitive environment.

Hanstad (2012) provided an excellent example of the subtleties in the choice facing the risk manager. He referred to the conundrum that confronted the Norwegian Winter Olympic team as it prepared for the 2010 Olympic Winter Games in Vancouver and evaluated the uncertainty of embarking on high-altitude training. On the one hand, there was the risk of illness when undertaking this type of training, due to exposure to a new environment. On the other hand, the team could potentially gain a competitive advantage over others by increasing the number of red blood cells, which are important in, for example, cross-country skiing. The response of minimising the risk of illness would mean that the team missed out on the opportunity to gain an advantage as a result of taking the risk.

Risk management as a concept has been around since the 1950s and was originally closely associated with the insurance industry. It subsequently expanded across a broad range of disciplines, including medicine, engineering and construction. When applied to projects, it systematically applies management policies, procedures and practices to identify, analyse, monitor and respond to project risk. The significance of project risk management increased as organisations began to manage their businesses in project mode. This is most evident in Project-Based Organisations (PBOs), where projects have become vectors of organisational strategy. It is only through effective management of a portfolio of projects and close alignment of their objectives with business strategy that project risk can be harnessed to generate positive business outcomes.

With multiple projects operating across the organisation, PBOs developed new organisational structures, revised accountabilities and responsibilities, and improved management decision-making. The way in which project risk is perceived and managed at all levels of an organisation is critical for organisational success. This requires a Project Risk Governance approach to integrate corporate and project risk activities.

While risk management is a well-developed discipline at the project level, the same cannot be said for the governance level. This book provides knowledge and guidance on managing project risk, both of a negative and positive nature, beyond the project level. The objective is to manage uncertainty through the implementation of value-protecting strategies, while taking advantage of opportunities through value-creating strategies, as a function of project risk governance.

Dieter Fink

Introduction

Renn (2010) was correct: 'Today's society seems to be preoccupied with the notion of risk.' In the past decade the world has seen the dramatic collapse of large organisations such as Enron® and WorldCom, and witnessed, more recently, the global financial crises, all drawing attention to the failures of effective risk management and the consequential substantial losses incurred by society. The response of legislators in the US and elsewhere was to draft laws that seek to enforce good corporate governance, including risk management.

The emphasis on risk control and compliance with law is now being extended to one that views risk management as a strategic corporate activity. Ernst & Young (2012) termed this mature risk management practice. There is a high level of integration and coordination across risk control and compliance functions, with an additional emphasis on turning the existence of risk into positive business results. Ernst & Young go so far as to conclude from their research that

> Risk is now becoming the fourth dimension of business. People were the first dimension. Process became the second dimension during the height of the manufacturing era. Evolving technology formed the third dimension. Embedded risk as the fourth dimension of business has the potential to fundamentally transform how organizations connect risk to reward.' (11)

Projects and Governance

As the perceptions of, and attitudes to, risk management change, new approaches to managing projects are appearing, largely brought about by the emergence of the Project-Based Organisation (PBO). Organisational objectives are now increasingly implemented through projects. Vertical bureaucracies are flattened in favour of teams and team-based arrangements. They are better suited to responding to fast-changing markets and meeting consumer needs. 'In PBOs, a project is a major endeavour and the mechanism for creating, responding to, and executing new business opportunities' (Peltokorpi and Tsuyuki 2006: 38). These developments have caused a review of the traditional positivist view of project management, with its well-defined tools and techniques for managing individual projects, offered by sources such as the Project Management Institute (PMI) and the Project Management Body of Knowledge (PMBOK®).

Within such organisations the challenge is not only to choose the right projects and deliver projects successfully, but also to ensure that projects can be sustained. The organisation has to continue finding projects that deliver new capacities and capabilities and contribute to profits. This falls within the scope of *Project Governance*: the forecasting and monitoring of the impact of project performance on overall organisation performance (Abu Hassim et al. 2011).

The concept of project governance is only beginning to be explored by practitioners and researchers. It has attracted many interpretations. One is to distinguish between the *performance* and *conformance* dimensions of governance. Performance provides expectations about the achievement of corporate objectives and is associated with operational activities such as effective resource utilisation in order to maximise the benefits flowing to stakeholders. Conformance, on the other hand, focuses on meeting the expectations of external scrutiny through compliance with various laws and principles. While conformance focuses on accountability and responsibility to demonstrate due diligence under law, performance has a leadership role linked to the execution of business activities and therefore has more a business orientation.

For project governance this means following acceptable and defensible industry standards and/or best practice and implementing internal systems that guide the operation of projects to achieve satisfactory business outcomes. Within project governance can be found *Project Risk Governance* (PRG), an even newer concept. Project risk governance is defined in this book as deploying organisational structures, processes and relational mechanisms that not only minimise the uncertainty associated with negative project risk but also maximise the benefits of positive project risk. Kendrick (2004: 69) referred to this as 'an organization's ability to manage risk as both a value-creating opportunity as well as a value-protecting activity'.

Project Risk Governance

To develop a PRG approach is challenging for a number of reasons. There is the need to integrate project risk with organisational risk activities. Tensions may arise because of the inherent need for flexibility and responsiveness (for example to react to new customer demands) as compared to the traditional, more static, corporate management approach. A more dynamic risk management approach is therefore required including the capability to quickly adapt projects to business conditions while still monitoring the overall risk environment. PRG is further complicated by the nature of risk itself (for example, it can be positive or negative) and the risk management capabilities of the organisation.

While it is recognised that knowledge about PRG is still in its infancy, a number of issues became apparent when researching and writing this book. They are associated with the key objective of this book, namely recognising the objective of PRG as value-protecting and value-creating. These themes will become apparent to the reader and are reflected in the following governance activities:

- aligning business and project strategy by taking into account project risk objectives, particularly those of positive risk;

- developing a project portfolio that achieves a risk profile acceptable to the organisation;

- constructing a business case for project investments that recognises the impact of risk on value-protecting as well as value-creating strategies;

- designing relational mechanisms in the form of steering committees and the Project Management Office (PMO) to link PRG processes and structures;

- adopting best practices in strategic and project management to provide a high level of PRG performance;

- referring to maturity models to guide the organisation to achieve a high level of PRG sophistication;

- providing organisational leadership from the board of directors downwards when executing PRG responsibilities.

The Objectives of this Book

This book examines risk management in modern organisations, particularly those that are project-based, through the lens of governance. In essence, it develops PRG principles that outline strategies to integrate business risk activities with project risk activities to ensure overall organisational success. Insights and guidance are provided on their design and implementation.

The second objective is to view PRG as having the dual objectives of value-creating and value-protecting. The book seeks to stress the management of positive risk by providing a roadmap that will ensure that the opportunities created by taking on project risk are successfully exploited.

To meet the above objectives, the book identifies and analyses relevant issues, provides insights into the topic and offers guidelines on how best to meet PRG responsibilities. It does so by addressing the following core questions:

1.   How are projects managed within organisations?

2.   Why is project risk management a governance responsibility?

3.   How do project and corporate risk activities interact?

4.   What are the PRG processes and structures that guide the organisation?

5.   What are the contextual factors that influence PRG?

6.   How is risk best managed at the project level?

7.   What steps need to be followed to reach PRG maturity?

The Design of this Book

The content of this book covers what is referred to in the profession as the 'front end' of project management (Morris 2009). Topics relate to governance, strategy, value management and building enterprise-wide PRG capabilities. As such, it reflects the 'governance' school of thought in project management (Bredillet 2008). The quality of the management of risks in the project portfolio, programmes and projects is determined by the effective governance performance of the board of directors, project sponsors, project managers and the PMO. Elements of the 'success' school of thought are included as they identify factors critical to the success of projects and PRG. Drawing on the 'behaviour' school of thought, the book outlines human resources management practices relevant to the transient nature of projects within project-oriented organisations.

The chapters are designed to provide a logical flow of issues related to PRG. They first examine the role of projects in organisations and the need to integrate project and business strategy within the framework of the project-based organisation. Next, PRG is introduced via its links with corporate and project governance. The scope of PRG is covered in two chapters that identify relevant processes, structures and relationship mechanisms. Contextual influences on PRG are recognised in the following chapter and cover a broad range of issues, from the professionalisation of project management to paradigmatic implications for its practise.

The 'back end' of PRG is covered in a chapter that identifies the essential requirements for managing risks at the project level. This is preceded by a chapter that gives insights into the concept of project risk to increase the reader's understanding of uncertainty, risk events, probabilities and so on. In a recent study by the author (Fink 2012), Australian project managers rated 'understanding the risk concept' as the number one key issue that confronts them. To assess the sophistication in current approaches and enable improvements to be made, the final chapter provides a roadmap along the stages and dimensions of a PRG maturity model.

The Benefits of this Book

This book is unique for two reasons. First, it places project risk management in the context of today's organisations, in which objectives are increasingly implemented through projects to better respond to fast-changing markets. Second, it applies a governance perspective to examine project risk at the project and corporate levels, an approach which is significantly under-researched and for which theoretical knowledge and professional practice are at an early stage of maturity.

By following the recommendations contained in this book, there is greater certainty of gaining value from exploiting project risks in project investments while, at the same time, reducing project failure by controlling project risks. Issues in achieving these outcomes are identified, thereby increasing the reader's understanding and his/her ability to influence project outcomes in a positive manner. Importantly, by applying the checklists provided in the book, the reader is able to self-assess the maturity of his or her PRG environment. Where self-assessment reveals a broadly unsatisfactory response this is a clear indication that the organisation needs to conduct further investigations.

The book makes a contribution to meeting the need for increasing the number of effective and risk-savvy project management professionals at all levels within the organisation. As stated in the Australian publication *Project Manager* (2012), 'good project managers will buck unemployment trends' and, more importantly from the perspective of this book, 'the hunger for project management basics, in particular risk management, will continue to surge'.

Suggested Audience

As this book draws on theoretical concepts, as well as professional practice, it is eminently suitable for a wide audience. They include members of boards of directors and senior management charged with responsibilities for corporate, project and risk governance. Their advisors will also benefit since the topic of PRG is covered across horizontal (within projects) as well as vertical (within organisations) lines.

At the project level, project sponsors will gain clarity on how project risk activities interact with those at the corporate level. This should give them confidence in making the right investment decisions and measuring project performance. Project managers and project risk managers will gain insights into the tools and techniques that are most critical to completing projects successfully.

Students and researchers interested in corporate governance, project governance and risk governance will benefit from this book. They are provided with a synthesis of the underlying literature, both academic and professional, and given insights into how theory is reflected in practice. In addition, the listed references provide further depth should the reader wish to learn more about a specific topic.

1

Projects in Organisations

Introduction

The common business model is highly structured, stable and predictable. Well-defined lines of responsibility and authority exist, usually organised in a hierarchical manner. A change is occurring as projects become a major component of organisational activities. According to Bredillett et al. (2008, referenced in Aubry et al. 2010), World Bank data shows that 21 per cent of the world's gross domestic product is tightly related to projects. To take maximum advantage of projects, vertically structured organisations are flattened so that they can respond quickly and efficiently to fast-changing market conditions. Old-style bureaucracies are increasingly being replaced by flexible, project-oriented structures.

Project- versus Product-Based Organisations

The questioning of traditional organisational arrangements has resulted in a preference for project-based approaches. This new structure is termed the project-based organisation (PBO) or multi-project organisation, and first emerged in the 1990s. For a PBO, the project is the basic form for organising its operations. It is particularly suited for entrepreneurial action and innovation since the nature of projects allows the organisation to respond quickly to an emerging market opportunity.

The key dimensions that distinguish the 'project-based organisation' and the 'product-based organisation' are business operations, technical processes and organisation structures (Du and Shi 2007). From a project management perspective, the key differences of the PBO when compared with product-based organisations are in the following two areas. First, production only occurs when the order is received and hence the project itself has to be flexible in the way it responds. For example, it may need a skillset different from previously completed projects. Second, high-level decisions have to be made as to whether or not to go ahead with the project. Projects compete with each other for funds and other resources within a portfolio of projects. To be included, the project has to contribute a net benefit to the organisation.

Table 1.1 highlights a number of differences that distinguish project-based from product-based organisations. In the former, projects are initiated and completed in agreement with the customer. They are made-to-order at a negotiated price and require a variety of skills, since each project is unique. The organisation structure is flexible and responsive to market needs, but concerns exist about the temporary and impermanent nature of the work. Product-based organisations, on the other hand, make stock for their inventory from which customers are supplied and charged according to a published price list. Production is largely automated and requires specialised skills. The organisation structure is hierarchical and recognises functional units and their strategic objectives.

Table 1.1 **Dimensions of product-based organisations and project-based organisations**

Dimensions	Project-Based	Product-Based
Production	Make-to-order	Make-to-stock
Demand	Unpredictable	Predictable
Volume	Low	High
Price	Negotiated	Fixed
Output	Customised product	Standard product
Delivery	On completion	From inventory
Process	Negotiated	Mechanical
Skill	Variety	Specialised
Organisation structure	Flexible, integrated	Fixed, hierarchical
Strategy	Add business value	Achieve business efficiency

While the PBO has the advantage of flexibility, it has a number of weaknesses compared to product-based Functional Matrix Organisation (FMO). Where there are multiple and unique projects, business costs are higher since there is little scope for routine work and hence a lower average cost of production. Each project potentially presents new technological and skill challenges for which little corporate memory exists. The dynamic nature of project work consistently exposes the project team to new environments. It is easier within an FMO than within a PBO to co-ordinate resources because of the high level of production predictability and centralised control. Within a PBO projects often run quite independently and parallel with each other and may compete for the same skills and financial resources. The allocation of scarce resources across projects will have to be determined by their projected contribution to business value, a difficult task.

FMOs tend to conduct centralised activities such as research and development (R&D) that benefit the organisation as a whole. This is generally lacking within PBOs since the organisation has been flattened so that it can respond quickly and efficiently to fast-changing market conditions. More emphasis is placed on 'eyeballing' the market than on internal activities. In a similar way support functions such as human resource management, finance and accounting, and legal services may receive less attention within the PBO than within the FMO.

An interesting approach is to classify types of projects by their broad governance paradigms. According to Mueller (2009) three paradigms can be identified. The 'conformist' paradigm requires that projects strictly comply with existing processes and rules. Experienced project managers are needed to decide the processes that will deliver the most economic results, i.e. the lowest cost possible. The paradigm applies to projects that are relatively homogeneous and subjected to tight regulations, such as can be found in the construction industry.

The 'versatile artist' paradigm requires a balancing of a diverse set of project requirements arising from the particular needs of different stakeholders. Organisations working with heterogeneous projects, such as those applying leading-edge technology, use this paradigm. Versatile and experienced project managers are needed to manage this dynamic environment.

Under the 'agile' paradigm, projects have a core functionality to which features are progressively added. The project sponsor prioritises the components of the project to be developed. An example is a software development project where the core is available for immediate use and additional modules are added over time.

The Project-Based Organisation

The PBO has characteristics that require excellence in project management at both the project and corporate levels. Aubry et al. (2007: 332) referred to this as 'a new sphere of management' under which corporate objectives are implemented through projects if the organisation is to maximise its business value. To achieve this aim, Peltokorpi and Tsuyuki (2006) recommended that PBOs adopt project-type processes throughout the organisation. These processes follow the traditional project stages of creating, responding to, and executing business opportunities.

DEFINITIONS AND FEATURES

The terminology used to define PBOs tends to accentuate the importance of projects. Among them are the following:

- Organisational project management: transforming the organisation by adopting a strategy to manage 'by projects'.

- Project business: the part of the business that directly or indirectly uses projects to achieve business objectives.

- Managing by projects: a corporate approach to project portfolio, programme and project management.

- Project portfolio management: managing the synergies between multiple projects, thereby adding value to the organisation.

- Temporary projects: projects are created to implement the organisation's strategy and, once accomplished, they are superseded by new projects.

The above definitions indicate that PBOs are a relatively new phenomenon and therefore pose new challenges to management. They will have to understand the implications of becoming a PBO, and its advantages and disadvantages. New dynamism is introduced since business strategy and project management closely interact to meet challenges in the environment. Emphasis is placed on realising new values for the organisation by gaining competitive advantages (e.g. by being first to the market) and innovation (e.g. by releasing new products and services).

While most attention is focused on strategic projects, PBOs also include non-strategic projects such as compulsory projects (e.g. in banks to install ATM systems to remain on par with competitors) and project maintenance activities (e.g. to fix errors in an IT system). They mostly do such projects for themselves rather than for external customers or entities. The distinction between internal and external is in aligning corporate and project strategies. With the former, the responsibility rests within the PBO, while for the latter the responsibility is that of the client.

THE PBO AND PROJECT PORTFOLIO

Attempts to manage projects from an organisational perspective have traditionally been done via the project portfolio. What distinguishes a PBO from project portfolio management is the close alignment within a PBO between the strategy of the business and that of the projects the strategy initiates. In other words, within PBOs corporate objectives are implemented through projects. Aubry et al. (2007) refer to this as the transformation of the organisation. The business now supports a dynamic and tight interaction between business strategy and organisational structure, which is now project based.

By contrast, under project portfolio management, the value generation potential is limited to the value added to the organisation by the synergy that is created between multiple projects. Emphasis is placed on the aggregation of projects making up the portfolio and how they are planned, managed and monitored. The responsibility for the project portfolio is that of senior management who implement and maintain processes and communications relative to the aggregate portfolio. With traditional project portfolio management there is little interaction with organisational strategy.

CORPORATE AND PROJECT ACTIVITIES

Aubry et al. (2007: 330) viewed a project-oriented firm as 'a dual set of functions: one of governance and one of operational control'. The governance perspective is reflected in the desire to align corporate and project activities to maximise business outcomes while control is exercised at the project level. Governance requires organisation-wide processes and structures to ensure that project potentials are strategically exploited. Control over projects serves to meet cost, time and quality objectives.

Tensions may emerge between corporate and project activities. Aubry et al. (2007) attribute this to friction and failure between the project and the organisation due to differences in what is expected of the project. Within PBOs there is a high expectation of gaining economic benefits from projects, which projects may subsequently fail to deliver. The solution appears to lie in managing expectations. Various options exist, including to 'under-promise and over-deliver', but this will increase the expectations for the next project. It may be best to 'deliver exactly what is promised, every time'. Promises need to reflect reality as perceived by both organisational and project management.

The PBO structure supports unique and transient projects. Novel processes are followed because products made or services provided are 'bespoke' for the beneficiaries of the project (Turner and Keegan 2001). This is in contrast to the traditionally managed firm that works well if markets, products and technologies are slow to change. Mass production dominates because of stable customer requirements and a slowly changing environment. It can be said that the organisation works like a machine, unlike a PBO.

In PBOs, it is important to retain some central functions but they have to be linked into the project networks. They are referred to as support activities and include human resource management, information technology and systems, accounting and finance, and legal services. Projects draw on their support and services as required but do not have direct responsibility for or authority over them.

Implications of Project-Based Organisations

When considering the transformation to a PBO, a range of implications should be evaluated for their impact.

UNPREDICTABILITY

The arrival of projects is stochastic; they are difficult to predict because they arise in response to market needs. This complicates business planning with its long-term view of the environment and the opportunities it offers. Projects in a dynamic market environment cannot be planned with confidence as to their frequency and timing. This has a number of implications. For example, with the possibility of multiple projects under consideration at any one time, project managers may be expected to supervise more than one project, or it becomes increasingly difficult to always have the right level of project skills available at any one time.

PROJECT REQUIREMENTS

For project managers, the rapid growth in projects within the organisation poses resource challenges. Project managers may have to come to an arrangement with each other to share limited organisational resources. There could be competition for scarce project talent. Agreement will have to be reached as to how best to allocate employees across projects taking into consideration their skill levels and those that are required. Each project will have to make its own case to gain a share of the resources available in the organisation.

EXPECTATIONS

The role of project managers is broadened as they are now closely entwined in the operations of the business itself. They are not only expected to be effective technically in the discipline of project management but also to have the necessary aptitudes to integrate the project within broader business activities. Success of projects determines the survival and future prosperity of the organisation. Expectations are further broadened when projects extend beyond organisational boundaries. When establishing a supply chain project, for example, the needs of both supplier and customer have to be considered.

BUSINESS MODEL

The challenge for the organisation is to design a business model that best suits itself. Options range from a pure PBO to one that also includes elements of the traditional functional and/or matrix organisational structure. The decision on the best configuration is determined by the number and nature of the projects. Should the volatility of projects be large then the emphasis would be on a pure PBO structure, while the reverse would apply for projects that are infrequent and similar. The greater the number and diversity of projects, the more pronounced are the characteristics of a PBO.

Advantages of Project-Based Organisations

There are a number of advantages associated with the PBO approach to conducting business.

OPPORTUNITY

As indicated earlier, by its nature a PBO offers increased opportunities for creativity and innovation. The organisation's products and services and project management processes are improved because of the close interaction between business strategy and project activity. Business strategy determines the changes needed to meet market needs while project management satisfies those needs through the completion of projects. Both interact to increase business value.

RESPONSIVENESS

The nature of projects allows a high degree of flexibility and responsiveness. In its simplest form, each project is a temporary endeavour to produce a unique product or service. It is a new undertaking and covers new ground. Not surprisingly, projects are staffed by professionals who are attracted by the dynamic nature of project work and exposure to different knowledge and skills. They become experienced in responding to challenges that are new to the organisation and themselves.

KNOWLEDGE MANAGEMENT

Knowledge management becomes important because of the rate at which project knowledge is created. Superficial or ineffective knowledge management causes opportunities to be missed or to be under-exploited. Project teams are encouraged to create 'lessons learned' repositories in which they carry forward their experiences and knowledge to subsequent projects, thereby improving the overall standard of project performance. The PBO itself benefits from an emerging knowledge culture as knowledge sharing and transference become pervasive.

EFFECTIVENESS

The design cycle required for new products, services and processes is completed more efficiently and effectively. The structural flexibility of PBOs facilitates the allocation of physical and human resources to endeavours that are of most benefit to the organisation.

In addition, PBO structures circumvent the traditional barriers to organisational change which require formal planning and change management. Projects benefit from well-established project management processes and the greater availability of project management expertise in comparison to scarcer change management skills.

Complexities of Project-Based Organisations

While there are clear advantages that can be identified for PBOs, there are a number of complexities that should be considered.

IMPERMANENCE

The temporary nature of a project introduces potential concerns among managers and employees. Perceptions of impermanence and discontinuance go against the human desire for stability and certainty. As projects will vary in length and number, predictions about future employment conditions are virtually impossible. Requirements for project staff can undergo substantial variations, causing volatility of the working environment. Even for activated projects, decisions can be made to change the scope of the project or even to terminate it at short notice should the expected benefits not materialise.

KNOWLEDGE

The emergence of numerous projects, often quite diverse in nature and loosely connected, makes project knowledge complex. Landaete (2008) sees this as a paradox for PBOs: faced with expectations of having knowledge to identify new and innovative endeavours, project teams rely on exploiting knowledge gained from previous projects. The concern is about the extent to which project knowledge gained from completed projects is useful in identifying and completing new projects.

BEHAVIOUR

Knowledge management may be weakened further by certain traits of human behaviour. Being given greater autonomy over projects due to the increased responsibility to integrate project and business activities, project managers may want to keep a competitive advantage by being less prepared to 'give up' the knowledge that they are gaining. Negative behaviours among project teams may also show up, such as free-riding and knowledge hiding.

REFLECTION

A lack of caring about issues outside the present projects may arise. Projects are often fast-paced (to meet market needs) with a fluctuating workforce (due to inability to predict the number of projects), leaving little time or willingness for reflection on the experiences gained and how they could benefit other projects. The risk arises that the 'wheel' is unnecessarily re-invented over and over again.

ALIGNMENT

PBOs have to manage the relative short-term objectives of projects with long-term organisational objectives. Complexity is introduced by multiple projects running sequentially and/or concurrently and requiring alignment with each other as well as with broader organisational activities. PBOs tend to lack the incentives and formal structures required for strategic management that can be found in traditional organisations.

Checklist: Understanding the Characteristics of a Project-Based Organisation

- Are multiple projects operating simultaneously within the organisation?

- Are projects regarded as the basic form of organising operations?

- Are projects expected to add creative and innovative capacity?

- Are projects seen to add business value?

- Are the differences between a project- and product-based organisation understood?

- Are projects of a temporary nature?

- Is the organisation structure regarded as flexible?

- Are the disadvantages of flexibility, such as lower economies of scale, accepted?

- Are projects of a heterogeneous nature?

- Is there excellence in project management?

- Is organisational strategy implemented through projects?

- Is the project portfolio closely aligned with business strategy?

- Are the implications of a PBO understood?

- Is a system of project governance implemented?

- Are tensions between project governance and project management resolved?

- Are some central functions, such as IT support, retained?

- Is it recognised that the arrival of projects is stochastic?

- Is the competition for resources between projects resolved?

- Do project activities extend beyond the organisation's boundaries?

- Are there elements of a traditional and/or matrix organisational structure?

- Are projects staffed by professionals who are attracted to their dynamic nature?

- Is project knowledge shared among project members?

- Are the consequences of the impermanence of projects on the project team recognised?

- Is there evidence of negative behaviour in projects?

- Is there time for reflection at the completion of projects?

Project-Based Organisation Structures

PBOs have traditionally been structured as a pyramidal organisation, also referred to as the 'contained' project management model (Thiry and Deguire 2007). With this configuration, they are simply 'replacing management rhetoric with project rhetoric' (Thiry and Deguire 2007: 651). By adopting the functional, top-down approach inherent in project management, the benefits of operating in project mode and aligning project strategy with business strategy are reduced. As the approach implies, there is a cascading structure from the board of directors downwards to individual projects, via the project portfolio and project programmes. The higher levels in the organisation determine the nature of the portfolio, identify programmes and approve projects for development. As shown in Figure 1.1, there is one portfolio, a small number of programmes within the portfolio, and a number of projects within each program. Synergy is created between projects but not between business and project strategy.

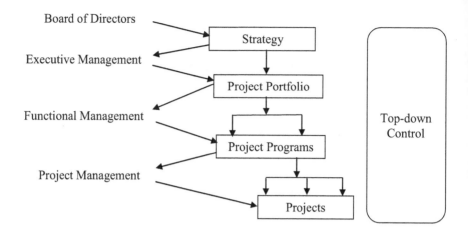

Figure 1.1   Pyramid structure of a project-based organisation

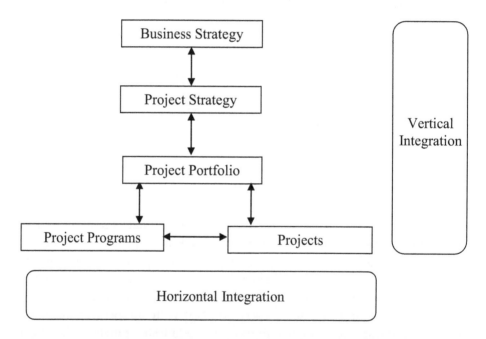

Figure 1.2   Integrated structure of a project-based organisation

To function effectively, a PBO demands dynamism and flexibility in the way programmes and projects link upwards with business strategy. Hence, there needs to be collaboration between project and organisational management.

However, according to Thiry and Deguire (2007) this aspect has not been sufficiently explored within the PBO environment. To remedy the situation, there should be horizontal and vertical integration processes that link business and project activities in the context of the PBO. Horizontal integration would ensure the completion of the project life cycle, while vertical integration would tie project activities to corporate strategy. Figure 1.2 provides a conceptual view of this approach. It is further developed in the following chapters.

Introduction to Project Risks

Risk at times has attracted attention only when projects fail. The importance of projects to the success of organisations, however, has shifted the focus to a proactive approach to project risk management. There are two essential prerequisites for this to be effective: understanding the nature of project risk and possessing the necessary risk management capability. The following is an introduction to these important concepts.

RISK EXAMPLES

At this point it suffices to think of project risk as an uncertain event or condition that, if it occurs, has a positive or negative effect on the project's objectives. Risks come from a wide variety of sources and can be both internal and external to the project. One could think of many examples:

- People risk. Projects are carried out by people and their performance largely determines the success or failure of a project. It is critical that the right skills are present on the team to bring the project to completion, team members are available when the project demands this, and the team understands the project's purpose and objective so that everyone pulls in the same direction.

- Organisational risk. There are many dimensions within organisations that should be considered. An example of project risk is the absence of stakeholder involvement. Since projects affect many stakeholders, they should be in agreement with the project and its purpose. A lack of consensus heightens the possibility of resistance to change. All relevant stakeholders should participate in initiating and completing the project so that it becomes their project and they take ownership of its success.

- Financial risk. Numerous financial risks could affect the project. For example, will currency fluctuations impact the availability of funds? Should the project be over a lengthy period, is ongoing funding available? Does the business case provide realistic estimates for project costs and benefits?

- Reputational risk. Activities and outcomes of projects can cause reputational damage should they not meet expectations. They involve mainly customers of the project who, if disappointed with the delivered product or service, will not provide a suitable future reference point. Reputation, like brand, can be destroyed quickly but takes a long time to re-establish.

- Legal risk. The organisation, operating through its projects, can potentially come into conflict with numerous governmental regulations and policies. Current high profile issues are occupational health and safety, the environment, and employment, privacy and consumer rights. To respond to these risks not only requires compliance with the law but also ethical conduct to act in the best interests of society.

A good example of organisational risk is the contemporary use of Information Technology (IT). Different types of risks can be identified with the use of technology:

- Business risk. By applying the 'wrong' technology, operational objectives may not be met and/or financial and market losses incurred. The acquisition of technology should be justified on the basis of supporting business activities and not for the sake of technology itself.

- Infrastructure risk. By not having available the most appropriate technology, the organisation will be at risk of becoming uncompetitive. Its competitors are able to offer better choices at better prices through the use of modern technology.

- Vendor risk. Risks are introduced should the supplier of technology not be able to maintain the operation of organisational systems. This will potentially cause breakdowns resulting in customer dissatisfaction and eventual business demise.

- Project risk. Technology has the reputation of cost and time overruns in its implementation for such reasons as relying on too-optimistic estimates and trying out new and unproven hardware and software.

- Staffing risk. The loss of staff with competence in managing complex technology is very disruptive. They may leave the organisation for a number of reasons, including being headhunted by another firm and/or feeling unrewarded.

RISK BREAKDOWN STRUCTURE

The Risk Breakdown Structure (RBS) helps to identify and define individual risk items. Its hierarchical design groups items under risk categories which vary from industry to industry and from organisation to organisation. An example of an RBS in which project risks are perceived as four categories (people, project management, finance and external) is provided in Figure 1.3. The RBS indicates concern about the competence and stability of people on the project team, the quality of project management, the adequacy of finance and the volatility of the external environment.

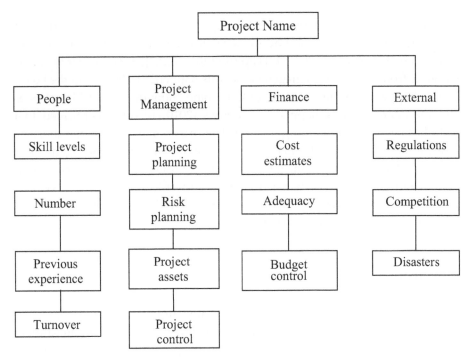

Figure 1.3   Example of a project risk breakdown structure

RISK MANAGEMENT CAPABILITIES

Risk management is well entrenched in central government bodies and highly regulated organisations such as banks, universities and telecommunication companies. Within government, bureaucratic decision-making processes ensure that there is high-level oversight and protection of the public interest. Risk management is used to prevent taxpayers' money being lost or squandered. Highly regulated organisations are subject to numerous laws and regulations and are obliged to report regularly on their risk management practices. 'Elsewhere, however, it has traditionally been viewed as a tiresome burden or overhead. Attitudes are now beginning to change – but slowly' (Everett 2011: 5).

It is tempting to perceive risk management as a costly activity and only give it attention when a disaster occurs and the organisation finds itself in trouble. At that stage the board and senior management may wish it had had the foresight, understanding and capability to implement adequate organisation-wide risk management. As the impact of project activities on corporate activities increases, so has greater attention to risks at the enterprise level, albeit slowly, it appears.

The concept of Enterprise Risk Management (ERM) has been around for years and boards are responding to its requirements, though apparently not sufficiently. Hermanson (2003: 42) captured this well: '[I]t seems that the focus has gone from "how did management let this happen?" to "how did the board let this happen?" In the future it could become "how did the ERM processes and the board let this happen?"' Moody's (2010) research confirmed that ERM has been slow in gaining traction. The reason may well be the shortage of experienced and well-trained board members and senior management in this area. 'Although risk managers play a crucial role in helping organisations understand both their own risk tolerance and risk appetite – a necessary precursor before any work in this area can begin – well-trained and experienced personnel are in short supply' (Everett 2011: 5).

Conclusion

This chapter has recognised the increasing importance of projects in generating economic activity and the consequent change in organisational structure. It contrasts the characteristics of project-based and product-based organisations, highlighting the important role that projects play in implementing organisational strategy. As PBOs are a relatively new phenomenon, various definitions are provided. The move to operating in project mode has implications, advantages, disadvantages and complexities. Among them is the stochastic arrival of projects, which provides opportunities but also introduces uncertainties. PBOs can be managed as a pyramid structure but more effectively when their processes are horizontally and vertically integrated. The chapter concluded by introducing the concept of project risk and the required risk management capabilities.

Example of Projects in ABC University

This example illustrates the significant role that projects play in ABC University. ABC University is an entirely fictitious entity but it can be argued that its characteristics are not uncommon among universities in the western world.

ABC University continues to experience major changes, a trend that has been accelerating in recent years. The major cause is that the funding it receives from public sources has reduced significantly as the principle of 'user pays' becomes more established within government, reflecting the view that 'why should the taxpayer fund the education of a small group of citizens?' With dwindling support, the university has to look at other sources of revenue. An obvious response is to increase the fees charged to students. With increasing tuition fees, students in turn have become more selective in how they choose the institution and the courses in which they enrol. These have to appeal to students and provide 'value for money'. ABC responded in a number of ways, and these are reflected in the project activities it undertakes.

One of the most noticeable aspects of ABC University has been its brand-building campaign. This is a project initiated by the marketing unit and involved surveying the public to establish current perceptions of the university's image and reputation. Creative activities developed an advertising theme that was deemed to best reflect the nature and ambitions of the university. The theme was integrated in advertisements of particular courses to strengthen its overall impact. The project will most likely continue for a number of years and its impact will be assessed in regular surveys. Different media are used, including traditional newspaper and television outlets and newer social media approaches that appeal more strongly to younger people who make up most of the student cohort. The major risk is the project's cost-effectiveness.

Financial pressures have also required the university's internal systems to become more efficient. A number of IT projects have been initiated to automate what were previously manual systems. Modern technology, especially the web, provides the means to link staff and students electronically and exchange information in a paperless format. One project is to link students, potential and current, with the university's website. The website provides a rich source of information, such as course material, and supports transactions, such as enrolling online in a particular course. Internally, another project has provided links between administrative and academic staff, via an intranet, to exchange information. One of the risks is the insecurity of web technology because it can be penetrated (e.g. to change stored data) and misused (e.g. to deface the university's home page) by those seeking to damage the reputation of the university.

There is an increasing expectation by students of being able to access their courses 'any time' and from 'any place'. More and more students are studying part-time to pay for increasing study fees and to progress their careers. Online education is therefore attractive to them and the university has responded. It has started a project that applies web software to offer its courses online. The mode of delivery is interactive since its approach seeks to replicate the lecturer–student relationship of the traditional classroom environment. Because of the use of leading-edge technology, project members have to have the required skill and experience to bring the project to a successful conclusion. A risk factor is the possible lack of the necessary expertise within the project team.

By adopting a client-oriented service approach, the university organises events for the public. The corporate affairs office is responsible for open days, information evenings and event sponsorships. Each of them represents a project that takes place once or twice each year and has to be 'refreshed' every time it is executed. Open days are intended for prospective students and have to be engaging to attract their attention and presence. The university therefore organises entertainment at these events, such as the appearance of a music band, in addition to staff demonstrating the benefits of the courses they teach. Information evenings suit students intending to study part-time and are organised at well located, high quality function facilities. Again, the project team has to make all the necessary arrangements. Sponsorship of high-profile events, such as an international tennis tournament, strengthens the brand image of the university. The risks of the projects are that they are poorly executed and cause more harm than good.

ABC University engages in many other projects. Examples are developing new courses, partnering with an offshore institution to teach the university's courses, and constructing new buildings to house laboratories or lecture halls. All these activities are delivered in project mode and are in response to the demands of a competitive education market. Besides undertaking projects, the university maintains a functional structure that provides central support to its faculties as well as projects. These are human resources (payroll and staff wellbeing), legal services (to settle disputes), quality control (over its courses), and IT. ABC University can be perceived as a hybrid PBO.

2

Business and Project Interaction

Introduction

When business strategy is implemented through projects it requires project activities to be aligned with corporate activities so that project objectives reflect those of the business. Projects are expected to contribute to the performance of the organisation by delivering improved products and/or services. With the increasing importance of projects, greater attention is given to the impact of project risks on business outcomes. If they are of a negative nature, risk response strategies are developed for value-protecting. The existence of positive project risks, however, provides opportunities for implementing value-creating strategies.

Business Strategy Formulation

Strategy has been defined in many ways, since '[t]here is no single unifying theory of strategy with many strategic schools of thought' (Young et al. 2012: 889). From the management literature it can be deduced that strategy sets direction for the organisation. It does this by:

- developing a plan that integrates the organisation's goals and polices with a set of actions;

- defining the scope of the organisation and publicising it in the organisation's vision, mission and objective statements;

- considering a time span that covers strategy for the short, medium and/or long term;

- gaining advantages for the organisation so that it is successful in the industry vis-à-vis competitors;

- responding to market needs and exploiting market opportunities;

- focusing on investments that grow the existing business and have the potential to transform it in the long term;

- making efficient use of resources by fully utilising the organisation's assets;

- exploiting the competencies of its people when implementing strategies;

- satisfying stakeholders' expectations for improved products and services;

- meeting shareholders' expectations for positive returns on the funds they invested in the organisation.

TOOLS FOR STRATEGY FORMULATION

Management can apply a number of approaches to formulate business strategy. They include the following:

- SWOT analysis. As the name implies, this approach identifies Strengths, Weaknesses, Opportunities and Threats. Strengths and weaknesses focus mainly on internal capabilities, resources and skills which are required to deal with opportunities and threats that are present in the external environment.

- Product and service life cycle. The premise is that products and/ or services have a finite life cycle by passing through stages of emergent growth before declining. Managerial action may be able influence the rate at which they pass through each stage. The purpose of strategy is to position the organisation within the cycle.

- PEST analysis. This approach analyses Political/legal, Environmental, Socio-cultural and Technological factors.

Included in the analysis are government legislation, rates of unemployment, demographic characteristics and technological innovation.

- Competitive forces. This analysis assumes that, at any given time, the organisation is affected by a number of different forces from its environment and from competition and rivalry in the industry. Also considered are the power of suppliers and buyers, the threat of customers changing to another product or service, and the likelihood of new players entering the market.

- Internal and external value chain analysis. The former breaks an organisation's activities into primary activities (e.g. inbound logistics, operations, outbound logistics, sales and marketing) and support activities (e.g. administration, human resource management). External value chain analysis links the organisation's activities with those of its suppliers, customers and alliances.

- Critical success factors. This analysis identifies areas that must go well for the organisation to achieve its objectives. Management needs to be supplied with information that enables it to track the organisation's performance in these areas. The factors are small in number to indicate their critical importance.

- Gap analysis. This identifies skills, knowledge, competencies and capabilities that the organisation requires to execute its strategies and achieve its objectives. Current resources and capabilities are compared with required ones to establish gaps and remedies to overcome deficiencies.

Strategic planning includes identification and management of project risk. As stated by Kendrick (2004: 71): 'Risk management is not an option. It naturally occurs as part of the strategic planning process (e.g. in more advanced applications of SWOT and PEST analyses) so the question is not whether or not it occurs, but how well it is understood and undertaken.' This chapter will now outline how project risks are identified and aligned with business strategy.

Business and Project Strategy Alignment

In the past, the strategy formulation process was assumed to be highly ordered and neatly integrated within various organisational processes. The outcome was the strategic plan that presented the organisation's goals, policies and actions as a coherent whole. Guidance was provided by well-known frameworks such as Porter's dimensions of cost-leadership, differentiation and focus (Porter 1980), and the product analysis of stars, cash cows or dogs of the Boston Consulting Group (Pearce and Robinson 1997).

With an increasingly volatile environment, a more dynamic and entrepreneurial approach is needed to succeed in strategy implementation (Young et al. 2012). This is particularly relevant to organisations in which strategy is actioned through the execution of projects. However, it appears that organisations struggle in linking project activities with business strategy and not much guidance is provided in the current project management literature (Aubry et al. 2007). A holistic approach to business/project strategic alignment is required (Young et al. 2012) so that only projects aligned with strategic business objectives are approved, funded and prioritised for development.

One approach is to determine value measures at the project level and to link them to those of the organisation. Strategic initiatives of the project become aligned with the strategic activities of the corporation. Value is created by projects in the context of the organisation's mission and business needs and is defined in business terms such as cost optimisation, increased revenues and market share, and improved customer satisfaction. Figure 2.1 provides an example of the alignment between business and project strategy. It shows business strategy in four areas and how project strategies are matched to them. The first strategy is to maximise business opportunities through being creative and innovative. Projects that produce unique products or services meet this objective and will receive organisational support. For another objective, to use knowledge to gain operational improvements, projects will have to demonstrate that knowledge is shared between project members and a 'lessons learned' repository is maintained. Aligning project activities with business goals is a continuous process and should not be perceived as a one-off task.

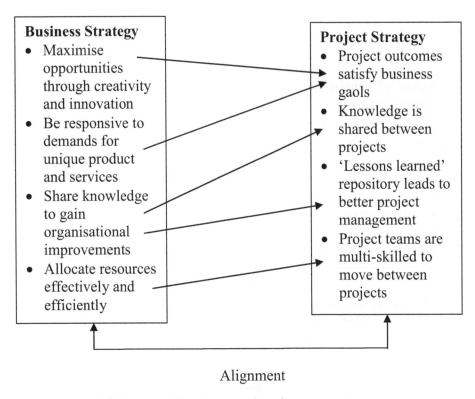

Figure 2.1   Alignment of business and project strategy

HIERARCHICAL AND CYCLICAL ALIGNMENT APPROACHES

The hierarchical approach to alignment is much used because it represents the traditional project manager's view of a functional and rational world. Business strategy is determined by top management and goals are cascaded down to projects. Figure 2.2 provides an example of value measures and delivery responsibilities. At the project management level, measures are about project management, project risk and project outcomes. Further up the hierarchy, project values are aligned with business operational values. An example is 'learning from experience' at the project level, which translates into 'sharing of knowledge' at the organisational level. It is at this stage that project management and business management have equal responsibilities for delivering expected values. When values are quantified in 'bottom line' terms at the highest level, value delivery is part of business management.

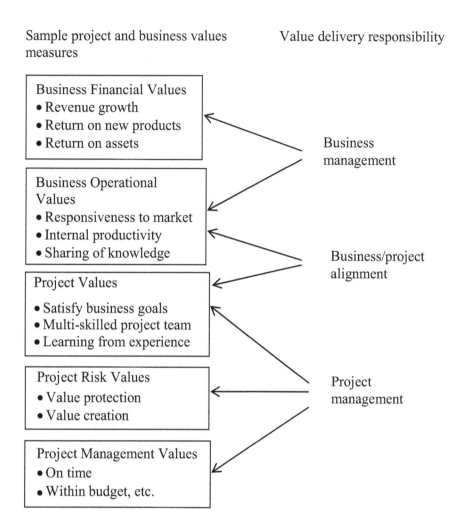

Figure 2.2   Hierarchy of business and project values

The hierarchical approach, however, is increasingly being discredited (Young et al. 2012) because it is based on a number of assumptions that do not reflect modern business. For example, it relies on a stable environment in which goals are predefined and strategy alignment can be achieved by following a relatively simple and objective process. This may no longer be the case in environments characterised by volatility and uncertainty, and in which alignment is facilitated rather than controlled.

The alternative approach to extracting business value from projects is to examine their life cycle. Du and Shi (2007) developed and tested a model for linking business strategy to project strategy via project portfolio and programme management. The model was applied within a large Chinese company that handled 80–100 projects of various kinds every year, including industrial and civil engineering, and highway and bridge constructions, costing millions of dollars. The model itself was considered by the authors as simple in concept but practical in application as well as complex in richness. They termed the four interrelated phases object ('what should do'), portfolio ('what can do'), decision ('how to do'), and action ('do it!').

When the concept is applied to business and project strategy, governance and management, Figure 2.3 emerges. Business strategy in the model determines what should be done within the organisation to maximise the opportunities provided by projects. The strategies are 'interpreted' to determine what can be done within the scope of project strategy. To guide the project, not only in managing the project but also to maximise its contribution to business success, project governance processes and structures come into play. They provide a high-level overseeing role for project activities. Project management itself implements strategy.

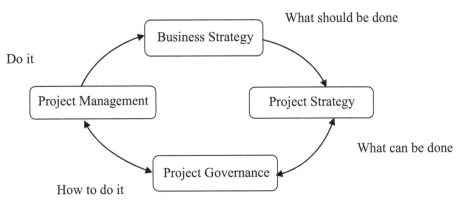

Figure 2.3   Cyclical approach to business/project alignment

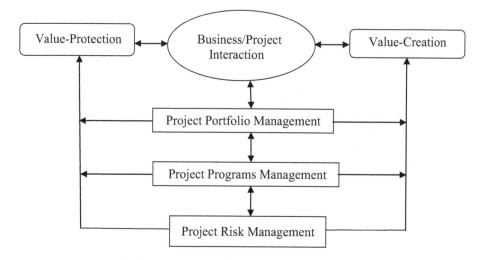

Figure 2.4   Alignment between business/project strategy and project risk management

There are various ways in which the generic cyclical approach can be adapted to suit the organisation and its environment. Hartman and Ashrafi (2004) incorporated the approach in their SMART™ project management framework. It aims to achieve a balance between business issues ('what are we trying to achieve?'), technology ('how are we going to do this?') and social issues ('who is involved and whom do we affect by the changes created by this project?'). SMART™ is an acronym for Strategic Management (the project needs to be of value to the sponsor organisation for it to be successful), Alignment (of stakeholders and the project team with the objectives of the project), Regeneration (a regenerative team that practises open communication and has a propensity to take risk) and Transitional (the ability to manage complexity, uncertainty, change and risk).

Alignment with Project Risk Management

Projects are now the key contributors to the performance of the organisation as they support the processes that deliver improved services and products. They are part of a structure that works as follows. Projects are grouped together to form a programme as sometimes it will take several projects to achieve a specific business goal. Building a road is a project, but only in conjunction with other projects that construct bridges and install a traffic management system will an effective transportation network be completed. Programmes in turn make up the project portfolio. The portfolio is the outcome of business/project strategy interaction and seeks to maximise the synergy that is created between the two.

From a risk management perspective, projects protect the organisation's existing values, such as its reputation, and/or create new values in the form of novel products and services. Project risks are identified at all levels but are progressively refined from the portfolio downward to the project level via project programmes. Without the vertical integration of projects, programmes and portfolio, the project manager would struggle to identify the value-protecting and value-creating roles that project risk plays. Figure 2.4 conceptualises the above arrangement.

Example of Aligning Business Objectives with Project Risk Management

Kaplan and Mikes (2012) provided an example of how strategic business objectives are formulated and aligned with project risk management. In the case of 'VW do Brasil' there were nine business objectives against which risks were identified:

1. Achieve market share growth.

2. Satisfy the customer's expectations.

3. Improve company image.

4. Develop dealer organisation.

5. Guarantee customer-oriented innovations management.

6. Achieve launch management efficiency.

7. Create and manage robust production volume strategy.

8. Guarantee reliable and competitive supplier-to-manufacture processes.

9. Develop an attractive and innovative product portfolio.

For each business objective, project risks were identified. For example, in respect of the project to meet the goal 'Satisfy the customer's expectations', eleven risks were found and assessed. Four of these risks were determined to be critical and required immediate attention or mitigation. The researchers did not provide details of their nature.

PROJECT RISK IDENTIFICATION

Literature and practitioner material provide comprehensive guidelines to risk identification. The nature of project risk, however, is complex and often misunderstood (see Chapter 8). As an example, a 'fact' is not a risk since risk is about uncertainty. The fact that there has been a crisis in the past does not necessarily mean that the crisis will occur again, even though some element of uncertainty exists. Furthermore, project risks by nature can be positive or negative. The team needs to be specific when determining what project risk is or is not, and its significance. What is also important is that the sooner risk is identified the better.

Project risks are identified to a large extent from existing documentation. First, the organisation's stated risk appetite and tolerance levels will determine the attitude to risk taking. Second, the project's mission and scope statements will define the sources from which risks may originate. Third, activities in other project management knowledge areas should be reviewed to identify possible risks within them. A superficial approach to project costing, for instance, may leave costs being ignored or wrongly estimated.

Project risk identification techniques are well known in the project management profession and include the following:

- Brainstorming. This technique is most often used when subject experts are involved. Those with the necessary experience and knowledge identify initial risk events and subsequently one idea spawns another. A suitable facilitator may be involved to start the process and guide the group in compiling a list of project risks.

- Checklist. The checklist is based on historical information and project experiences. It is useful for projects of a similar nature. Checklists are developed to a detailed risk level and refined at the completion of each project.

- Interviewing. Interviews are question-and-answer sessions where the team interviews subject experts, stakeholders, users and managers. The questions can be structured (requiring specific answers) or unstructured (more like a discussion). To guide the interview, teams often use the Work Breakdown Structure (WBS) to get interviewees thinking about risks in tasks required to complete the project.

- SWOT analysis. This approach is very popular and often practised. It requires the team to examine each of the Strengths, Weaknesses, Opportunities and Threats of the internal and external environments as they may affect project risks.

- Delphi technique. This is a sophisticated method in which experts are approached and asked to rate potential project risk via a questionnaire. Responses are organised by the mean rating for each item and sent back for further input, additions and comment. The experts are asked to consider the group's mean rating for each risk item and to modify it if they think it is necessary. After another round a fresh list is compiled with new ratings. After about three rounds consensus is reached among the group on the project risks that exist and their ranking.

- Assumptions analysis. Assumptions underlying predicted project risks are examined by exploring their validity for accuracy, consistency and completeness. Each project risk is tested for the strength of its assumption and redefined if an assumption turns out to be false.

Checklist: Aligning Strategy with Project Risk Management

- Does the alignment of business and project strategies give direction to developing project risk strategies?

- Are initial project risk strategies formulated during project portfolio management?

- Are project risk strategies progressively refined during project programme management?

- Are project risk strategies implemented during project management?

- Is the nature of project risk clearly understood?

- Are project documents accessed to establish the sources of project risks?

- Is the project team familiar with the techniques for identifying project risks?

- Are the techniques used to identify project risks adequate?

Strategies for Value-Protecting

Value-protecting strategies aim to prevent the loss of business value, or at least to preserve it. Value can be found in many diverse areas of business activity and varies from organisation to organisation and between industries. In the IT project field, for example, potential loss of business value is attributed to four types of risk: market risk, credit risk, operational risk and compliance risk (ISACA 2009). Illustrations for each can easily be found. Market risks materialise when the delivery of an inferior product or service causes the organisation's reputation to suffer. A project that consumes substantially more funds than originally estimated brings about financial hardship and a deteriorating overall credit rating. Operational risk can occur when project staff suddenly leave and there is no contingency plan to replace them. The project may have to be abandoned, creating the perception of unreliability. Compliance risks are brought about by ignorance of current laws and legislation and could result in penalties being imposed.

A generic approach to value-protection was recommended by Renn (2010). He identified four classes of risk problems and strategies to address them: linear (routine) risk, complex-induced risk, uncertainty-induced risk and ambiguity-induced risk. With linear or routine risks, value is protected by applying methods that are non-controversial and the remaining uncertainties are therefore low. An example is food risk. To protect food from deteriorating, the standard practice of storing it under refrigerated conditions should be adopted. There is little risk that the quality of food will be affected with this precaution.

With complex-induced risk, complexity is associated with the risk event and a possible cause-and-effect situation. Risk can only be reduced by receiving and processing complete information about its characteristics. An example is assessing the risk in building construction. Information is collected about events or conditions that can go wrong during construction through a cause-and-effect approach. Defective material, for example, may cause walls to crumble under extreme weather conditions. This information is used to establish building codes that, if followed, will protect the value of the completed building.

With uncertainty-induced risk, as the name implies, uncertainties are high and the full extent of the remaining risk is unknown. These risks require a cautionary approach, such as containment and making systems resilient, rather than seeking to remove risk entirely. Emergency systems have these characteristics since future risks are impossible to predict with certainty and may or may not be successfully managed during the emergency. For example, consideration is given to protecting infrastructure against extreme flooding, but this may only occur once in a hundred years. Despite raising dam levels and building bridges there is no assurance that these measures will be adequate when the emergency arises.

With ambiguity-induced risk, differing views are expressed about the nature of risks, i.e. their relevance, meaning, consequences and so on. These conflicting viewpoints need to be explored and reconciled. The example given by Renn (2010) is genetically modified agricultural products about which different opinions exist, from positive (e.g. improving the yield of products) to negative (e.g. the long-term impact of new technology being used). Farmers may be given the choice of adopting or not adopting genetic modification according to their risk appetite and tolerance levels.

Kaplan and Mikes (2012) identified three categories of risk that were, according to them, related to strategic choices and should be considered by organisations in their strategy formulation and implementation processes. The first two are value-protecting while the third is value-creating. Value-protecting strategies deal with preventable risks which arise from within the organisation and are controllable, and external risks that arise from events outside the organisation and hence are beyond its influence or control. However, their influence can be mitigated. Value-creating strategic risks are those where an organisation voluntarily accepts some risk in order to gain superior performance. They are not inherently undesirable and are key drivers to capturing potential gains.

STRATEGIES FOR PREVENTABLE RISKS

Preventable risks are defined as controllable and offer no strategic benefit from leaving them as they are. They are perceived as negative risks, can take many forms and can cover a wide range of activities as outlined above. Strategies that are effective in risk prevention focus on avoiding or eliminating them in a cost-effective manner. Kaplan and Mikes (2012) identified four value-protecting strategies: rules, standard operating environment, values and compliance.

Applying rules requires mapping the likelihood and impact of the risk and eliminating those that exceed a boundary value. An example of the approach is reflected in the cause-and-effect diagram.

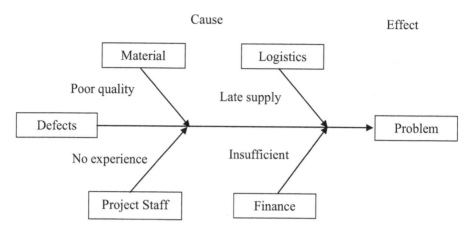

Figure 2.5   Cause-and-effect diagram

Figure 2.5 shows how various causes can be identified as causing a problem. 'Defects' with material, staff experiences and so on have caused the 'problem' with the project to occur. If the causes are judged to have a severe effect, the project would not be approved. To avoid a negative effect on the project, causes have to fall within established borders or rules. Material, for example, will have to meet certain quality specifications.

By introducing a Standard Operating Environment (SOE) it is possible to disallow operations outside the environment. This is especially effective in standardising computing hardware and software across projects within the organisation. Only nominated brands and models, carefully evaluated by an expert group, are approved and supported for use by the project team. Acquisitions outside the SOE require justification and approval by a higher-level authority. Problems, should they occur, remain the responsibility of the requisitioning body rather than that of a central body.

Another strategy is to develop a mission statement and value and belief systems that educate management and staff to be aware of and avoid preventable risks. The aim is to develop an organisation culture that clearly indicates to everyone 'what is not allowed'. Risk-averse attitudes are created through a programme of education, training and awareness. By improving risk awareness and developing skills and knowledge, preventable risks are recognised and responded to as a matter of urgency.

Compliance is achieved through implementing a system of internal controls and conducting regular audits. There are two types of control: managerial and operational. The former addresses the design and implementation of risk planning and risk management. Operational controls cover management activities such as responding to risks related to personnel and the physical environment and require lower-level planning, such as disaster recovery and incident response planning. Audit carries out risk management reviews to ensure that risk response processes are being followed correctly.

STRATEGIES FOR EXTERNAL RISK

External factors relate to the market/economy in which the organisation operates. They include the industry, its rate of change and latent competition, regulations and compliance requirements, and technology developments. Since their occurrence cannot be controlled, their impact should be reduced in a cost-effective manner when the event occurs. Risk response is in line with the defined risk tolerance of the enterprise and residual risk falls within risk tolerance limits. Strategies to manage external risks are described below.

Kaplan and Mikes (2012) recommend 'envisioning' external risks through tail-risk assessments and stress testing, scenario planning, wargaming and acting as devil's advocate. The approach of developing risk scenarios is well established in IT project management. 'It is a core approach to bring realism, insight, organisational engagement, improved analysis and structure to the complex matter of IT risk' (ISACA 2009: 51). Risk scenario components as they may apply to project risks are shown in Figure 2.6.

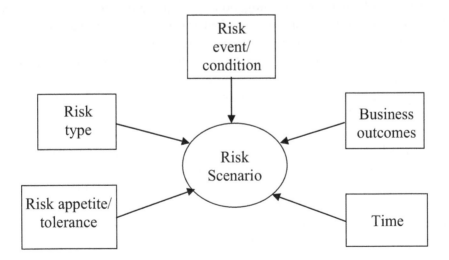

Figure 2.6   Developing project risk scenarios

A risk event or condition is one that, if it occurs, has a positive or negative effect on the project objective. It is usually assumed that risk is negative in that it is harmful to the project. However, risk can be positive and therefore supportive of project objectives. Project risks are strategically managed so that they support business outcomes in the form of new or improved products and services. The above components are considered by senior management in scenarios of various levels of organisational risk appetite and tolerance over different time periods. The longer the time, the greater is the uncertainty of the developed scenario. Risk appetite is the amount of risk an organisation is willing to accept in the pursuit of its mission, while risk tolerance is the acceptable variation caused by risk when accomplishing the mission.

Risk avoidance means not undertaking activities or bypassing conditions that give rise to risk. The strategy should be applied when no other risk response, such as sharing or transferring the risk, is adequate. Avoiding certain events or conditions reduces flexibility as there are fewer options available. A strict cost–benefit approach should be applied. The cost of implementing the response should not exceed the cost of repairing the damage. When the risk is being located in a flood-prone area, it can be avoided by changing the project location away from the area. This will eliminate the impact of a natural disaster event and protect the project objectives. Not every risk, however, can be avoided, and any residual risk should fall within the organisation's risk tolerance limit.

Under risk reduction or mitigation, strategies are followed that reduce the probability and/or consequences of an adverse risk event to an acceptable threshold. The more flexibility the project team has, the more valuable is this approach. A risk reduction strategy for projects in flood-prone areas is to have strong recovery procedures that will ensure that project activities resume quickly after a flood event. For example, the project team is relocated to alternative premises when the flood occurs.

The risk transfer/sharing strategy seeks to shift the consequence of a risk or portion thereof to a third party together with ownership of the response. It does not eliminate the risk, it just transfers/shares responsibility for the risk. Taking out an insurance policy or outsourcing project work are common examples of the strategy. The strategy protects the organisation against the financial consequences of an adverse risk event.

When no action is taken in response to the risk, a consequential loss is accepted if/when it occurs. It does not mean that the risk is ignored; an informed decision is made to accept the risk. Organisational management, both business and project, carefully consider this strategic option to managing risk. They have decided that the occurrence of a disruptive flood is 'a one-in-a-hundred-years' event and hence the risk should be accepted.

Contingency planning provides a response to risks that have not been identified and have no value-protecting strategies. In other words, an unforeseen risk event or condition occurs and the organisation activates its contingency plan. The main goal is restoration to normal modes of operation with minimum cost and disruption to normal activities. Contingency planning covers incident response planning, disaster recovery planning and business continuity planning.

Checklist: Do Project Risk Strategies Protect Organisational Value?

- Can values be identified for different organisational project activities?

- Are the sources and nature of these risks known?

- Have generic approaches been identified to respond to project risks?

- Is a distinction made between strategies for preventable and external project risks?

- Is there familiarity with strategies for preventable project risks?

- Are strategies for external project risks cost effective?

- How are external project risks envisioned?

- Are all potential project risk response strategies considered?

- Is there a contingency plan for unidentified project risks?

Strategies for Value-Creating

Opportunities for value-creating exist when the organisation is prepared to accept some risk in order to gain the advantage that is potentially available because of the existence of the risk. Kaplan and Mikes (2012) refer to the strategic nature of risks and point out that they cannot be managed through a rule-based control model. There are four generic strategies that can be applied to manage positive risks: risk exploitation, risk sharing, risk enhancement and risk acceptance.

Risk exploitation seeks to eliminate the uncertainty associated with a particular upside risk by making the opportunity definitely happen. The strategy does so by maximising the return offered by the opportunity. Risk exploitation means that more resources are allocated to the project that is perceived to offer a high value-creating outcome. The organisation is seen to 'grab' the opportunity on offer and is well aware of the potential positive outcomes.

When sharing a positive risk, part-ownership is allocated to a third party who is best able to capture the opportunity. This may be caused by a lack of internal resources or expertise which is available elsewhere. The organisation agrees to partner with another firm to realise the opportunity, albeit at a lower share of the outcomes for itself. Risk sharing is an option when a new product requires expensive manufacturing facilities beyond the organisation's financial means. The decision is made to share manufacturing and resulting revenues with the partner organisation.

Risk enhancement modifies the size of an opportunity by increasing the probability of occurrence and/or its positive impact. There is a deliberate increase in risk-taking with the view of increasing potential returns. The organisation may consider hiring project staff who have the ability to think creatively. Because they are scarce in numbers it uses a risk enhancement strategy and offers an attractive remuneration package. A strong demand for their talents means there is the risk that they could be headhunted by a competitor at any time. While they are working on the project, however, there is the opportunity to develop attractive new products or services.

Finally, there is an acceptance that positive risk is part of day-to-day project life. In other words, value and risk are two sides of the same coin. It is assumed that by letting the risk play out, resultant benefits emerge naturally. This can only happen when opportunities for value-creation are not lost by eliminating too many risks.

For the successful realisation of strategic risks, Kaplan and Mikes (2012) recommended engaging independent experts, facilitators and embedded experts. Independent experts represent expertise in business, project and/ or risk management from outside the organisation who are periodically engaged to review risk strategies. They act both constructively to complement shortcomings, and confrontationally as devil's advocates by initiating vigorous debate about positive risk strategies.

Facilitators are a small central risk management group within the organisation for projects to consult in developing risk strategies. By their nature they have an excellent overview of the whole organisation and are thus able to ensure that strategic risks are exploited for the overall benefit of the organisation. Embedded experts are members of the project team with strong expertise in risk management who continuously monitor the risk profile of the project. They are particularly relevant for high-risk projects in which risk situations can change dramatically. They work side by side with the project manager in seeking innovative, new ideas and exploiting the existence of positive risk.

Checklist: Do Project Risk Strategies Create Organisational Value?

- Is the difference known between positive and negative project risks?

- Does the organisation accept project risks to gain an advantage?

- Are all risk response strategies considered to exploit positive project risks?

- Are the opportunities of positive risks realised through engaging experts and facilitators?

Conclusion

This chapter introduced the important concept of strategy formulation and its role in developing business and project objectives. Strategies interact to provide the maximum benefits from operating in a project mode. Business strategies are matched with relevant project strategies through a set of business and project values. They can be aligned in a hierarchical or cyclical approach. Business/project strategy is further aligned with project risk strategies for the dual purpose of value-protecting and value-creating. A range of project risk response strategies is identified to prevent the loss of business value or realise the opportunities that project risks can provide.

Example of Business and Project Interaction at ABC University

This is a continuation of the fictitious example of ABC University. The university conducts a range of projects, some of which were outlined in Chapter 1. An indication was provided of how these projects support the university's objectives.

ABC University's core business is teaching and learning and research. In its teaching and learning activities, ABC has to balance a number of objectives. One is to satisfy the demand from students to be 'job ready' once they complete their courses. They expect to get a return on their 'investment' of time and money spent on studying. The teaching programme therefore has to impart technical skills, desired by employers, and provide industry experiences. The latter are typically gained during the teaching period in an appropriately termed 'industry project' unit to reflect work done by students for an outside client. The business objective of the university (getting students job ready) are aligned with those of the project (giving students skills and experiences). Both have a set of value metrics attached. For the university it is 'graduate employment', i.e. the rate at which its students find employment after graduating. For the course it is the satisfaction expressed by the client with the tasks performed by students.

A more subtle objective for ABC University is to instil the desire of life-long learning in its students. This will encourage them to come back to the University for further education over the following years. To motivate students requires excellence in teaching. The university has therefore developed programmes about effective teaching strategies. Each of these programmes is a project since pedagogical experts have to be consulted in their design and experienced facilitators identified to lead the programmes. The outcome of staff training should be reflected in positive student satisfaction surveys.

The second core mission of any university is to produce significant research outcomes. These are reflected in financial grants, publications in prestigious journals and being invited to consult to government or major organisations. Being successful in winning and utilising a research grant constitutes a project. There is the requirement to identify the team of researchers qualified to meet the grant conditions, the writing of the grant application, quality control to ensure that there remains no financial or legal exposure for the university, and submission. Should the application be successful, the research is completed in project mode. The achievement of its objectives is monitored, a budget is maintained and controlled, time schedules are prepared and so on. The university measures the value of grants by their number and size. For the researcher, who provides the project leadership, the measures are the prestige of the grant and the impact of the completed research.

The above are a few examples of how the university's strategy aligns with those of the projects it initiates. From a project risk response perspective each project has its own strategy. When developing the practicum project, the university seeks to protect its reputation as an educator with an applied approach. It faces a 'complex-induced risk' and therefore collects as much information as possible about the task students will perform for the client. This includes a precise scope of the work to be done and expected deliverables. In addition, information will be obtained about the time the academic supervisor can give to the project and to what extent the client is willing to engage with the students.

For the project to instil the desire of life-long learning, a value-creating approach is available. The opportunity exists to have recurrent students enrolling in courses provided the university takes on the risk of training its staff to become better at motivating its students. A 'risk exploitation' strategy is applied in which resources are spent on developing staff training programmes to 'grab' the opportunity that is available. The outcome of the project is perceived to be of high value since returning students sustain the operations of ABC University.

A 'risk sharing' strategy could be chosen when applying for a high-value research grant. Grant allocating bodies tend to favour applications that have been developed across a number of universities because it diversifies overall risk. Researchers in ABC University would therefore collaborate with researchers in other universities when submitting their application. This provides greater depth of research expertise but also requires sharing the rewards when winning the grant.

The above examples demonstrate how business and project strategies align and how project risk strategies can be applied to not only protect university values but also to enhance them.

3

Corporate and Project Governance

Introduction

The case of Enron® was one of the most dramatic examples of the need for effective corporate governance. Enron®'s downfall, as described by Zimmerman (2002) in *USA TODAY*®, was brought about, in broad terms, by overaggressive strategies combined with personal greed. The expectations for improved corporate governance have become very noticeable, especially in the United States where the Sarbanes–Oxley Act (2002) aimed to restore investor confidence in markets by imposing codes of conduct on corporations. More recently, in the wake of the global financial crisis, governance at the corporate level has again attracted attention.

With the increasing role that projects play in the success of organisations, management's attention is being drawn to their responsibilities in this regard. There is both external and internal scrutiny of the way projects are executed. Externally, the public has close contacts with the organisation and its governance through project activities. Internally, projects are the drivers of business success and create value for shareholders/stakeholders.

The Concept of Governance

The noun 'governance' is a derivative of the verb 'to govern'. According to Oxford Dictionaries (n.d.), 'govern' comes from the Greek word *kubernan*, which means 'to steer' – to guide or control the movement of, for example, a vehicle or a ship, or to direct/guide in a particular direction. 'Govern' may therefore mean to conduct the policy and affairs of a state, organisation or people; to control or influence; or to constitute a rule, standard or principle (Oxford Dictionaries n.d.).

Governance denotes the 'action or manner of governing' (ibid.). While action is the process of doing something in order to achieve a purpose, manner is the way in which something is done or happened. This is succinctly captured by Mueller (2009: 1): governance is about 'the conduct of conduct'. As will become apparent, governance includes two fundamental elements: processes (i.e. the action of governing) and structures (i.e. the way the organisation is designed), moderated by the behaviour of people (i.e. those required to perform or carry out the actions).

Governance can have an orientation anywhere between acting in the interests of shareholders or those of the stakeholder (Mueller 2009). Under the former theory governance seeks to maximise shareholders' returns on their investments when they take up equity in the organisation. It calculates these returns in financial numbers, typically as the 'bottom line' profit made by the organisation during the year. The board of directors and senior management are charged with the responsibility to act in the best interests of its shareholders. Project-based organisations have to take this into account when deciding on their project portfolio and project developments. A disadvantage of the shareholder theory of governance is the emphasis on short-term returns to satisfy shareholders' expectations of a dividend payout year after year.

The stakeholder theory of governance takes a broader view of investing in projects since the 'greater good' is considered. The organisation views itself as operating in a wider context, influenced by social expectations for being a good employer, and working with partner organisations to add value to the industry in which it operates. A stakeholder is any party that is affected by the gain or loss made on the project. When deciding on the portfolio of projects and project priorities, financial as well as other criteria are considered. They may be about the organisation's reputation, attractiveness as an employer, being a responsible citizen, and so on. Which of the two models is chosen, or where the organisation is located on the continuum, depends on its governance philosophy.

There are common elements across both theories:

- Objectives. Boards and senior management do not act in their own best interests but in those of outside parties, namely shareholders and/or stakeholders.

- Processes. The term 'govern' implies management's ability to implement policies and procedures that steer/guide the organisation to achieve its key objective of meeting the expectations of shareholders/stakeholders. Oversight and supervision ensure that governance processes are complied with.

- Structure. Direction and control are exercised within the organisational structure, typically headed by the board of directors and executive management. Other levels of management are usually represented in committee structures.

- Behaviour. The decisions and actions of boards and senior management are transparent and fully disclosed. They reflect a high ethical standard and corporate social responsibility.

- Performance. This is assessed by comparing business outcomes against strategic targets. Progress against plans is continuously measured so that corrective action can be taken should this be necessary.

Corporate Governance

Among the earliest versions of corporate regulations is the UK Code on Corporate Governance (also referred to as the Code), produced in 1992 by the Cadbury Committee. As stated by the UK Financial Reporting Council (2010), the code provided the classic definition of corporate governance:

> Corporate governance is the system by which companies are directed and controlled. Boards of directors are responsible for the governance of their companies. The shareholders' role in governance is to appoint the directors and the auditors and to satisfy themselves that an appropriate governance structure is in place. The responsibilities of the board include setting the company's strategic aims, providing the leadership to put them into effect, supervising the management of the business and reporting to shareholders on their stewardship. The board's actions are subject to laws, regulations and the shareholders in general meeting.

The concept of corporate governance became further formalised in 1999 when the Organisation for Economic Co-operation and Development (OECD) sought to promote its importance. The term, as described by OECD (2004), covers the following:

Corporate governance involves a set of relationships between a company's management, its board, its shareholders and other stakeholders. Corporate governance also provides the structure through which the objectives of the company are set, and the means of attaining those objectives and monitoring performance are determined. Good corporate governance should provide proper incentives for the board and management to pursue objectives that are in the interests of the company and its shareholders and should facilitate effective monitoring.

The OECD (2004) recognised that '[t]here is no single model of good corporate governance', but that '[t]he presence of an effective corporate governance system, within an individual company and across an economy as a whole, helps to provide a degree of confidence that is necessary for the proper functioning of a market economy'. It does so by specifying the distribution of rights and responsibilities among different participants in the corporation, such as the board of directors and management, providing the structure by which the company objectives are set, outlining the means of attaining those objectives, and monitoring performance. These are reflected in the principles of corporate governance outlined below.

PRINCIPLES OF CORPORATE GOVERNANCE

Among the many countries that have issued corporate governance reports are the following:

- OECD (2004): *Principles of Corporate Governance;*

- Australian Stock Exchange Corporate Governance Council (2010): *Corporate Governance Principles and Recommendations* (2nd edition);

- UK Financial Reporting Council (2010): *The UK Corporate Governance Guide;* and

- US Business Roundtable (2010): *Principles of Corporate Governance.*

Organisation for Economic Co-operation and Development

The corporate governance approach suggested by the OECD (2004) provides insights and guidance to its member countries at a macro level through the following set of six principles. They play a key role in ensuring good corporate governance practices and provide guidance on their implementation.

1. 'Ensuring the basis for an effective corporate governance framework.'
    The OECD (2004) recommends that the company promotes 'transparent and efficient markets' in which it operates and that they comply with the rule of law. It emphasises establishing clear lines of responsibilities among different levels of organisational management.

2. 'The rights of shareholders and key ownership functions.'
    Corporate governance practices should 'protect and facilitate the exercise of shareholders' rights'.

3. 'The equitable treatment of shareholders.'
    In addition to principle two, all classes of shareholders should receive equal treatment and have the right to have their concerns heard and resolved. Classes include minority and foreign shareholders.

4. 'The role of stakeholders in corporate governance.'
    Stakeholders are recognised as playing an important part in creating the organisation's wealth and jobs and sustaining its financial viability. The organisation should work with stakeholders to achieve these outcomes.

5. 'Disclosure and transparency.'
    Material containing important information should be disclosed in a timely and accurate manner. This includes information about the corporation's financial situation, performance, ownership and approach to governance.

6. 'The responsibilities of the board.'
    Three board responsibilities are identified: provide strategic guidance, monitor the performance of management, and be accountable to the organisation and its shareholders.

Australia

The Australian Stock Exchange (ASX) Corporate Governance Council (2010) provided recommendations that are intended to provide a reference point for companies about their corporate governance structures and practices. It is acknowledged that, in themselves, they cannot prevent corporate failure or poor corporate decision-making, but they are intended to lay a solid foundation for good management and oversight. There are the following eight principles:

1. 'Lay solid foundations for management and oversight.'
    This is achieved by establishing and disclosing the respective roles and responsibilities of the board and management.

2. 'Structure the board to add value.'
    Attention is given to the composition and size of the membership of the board and members' commitment to adequately discharge their responsibilities and duties.

3. 'Promote ethical and responsible decision-making.'
    This principle is self-explanatory.

4. 'Safeguard integrity in financial reporting.'
    There should be an approach such as using independent auditors to verify and confirm procedures that safeguard the integrity of financial reporting.

5. 'Make timely and balanced disclosure.'
    Information about the company that is considered of a material nature should be disclosed in a timely and balanced manner.

6. 'Respect the rights of shareholders.'
    Not only should shareholders' rights be respected but the company should facilitate their exercise.

7. 'Recognise and manage risk.'
    A sound system of risk oversight and management and internal control should be established.

8. 'Remunerate fairly and responsibly.'
    Attention is given to the nature of the remuneration paid so that its

composition and size is sufficient and there is a clear connection with the expected level of performance.

United Kingdom

The UK Financial Reporting Council (2010) recognised that '[t]he Code is not a rigid set of rules. It consists of principles (main and supporting) and provisions.' The UK adopted the 'comply or explain' approach as the trademark of corporate governance to ensure flexibility in its interpretation and application. The code addresses the following topics:

1. 'Leadership.'
    The board is responsible for the long-term success of the company but needs to distinguish between its board responsibilities and those of the executive in the running of the company's business.

2. 'Effectiveness.'
    For the board and its committees to carry out their duties and responsibilities effectively it needs to possess the appropriate mixture of skills, experience, independence and knowledge of the company. Directors should receive an induction on joining, regularly refresh their skills and knowledge, and undertake an evaluation of the board's performance.

3. 'Accountability.'
    Part of the board's responsibility, when assessing the company's position and prospects, is to determine 'the nature and extent of the significant risks it is willing to take in achieving its strategic objectives'. They should disclose in a formal and transparent manner their corporate reporting and risk management and internal control principles.

4. 'Remuneration.'
    Levels of remuneration should be adequate to attract directors of quality, but not excessive. A significant part of the package should be linked to corporate and individual performance and be determined by transparent policy and procedure.

5. 'Relations with Shareholders.'
    It is suggested that the Annual General Meeting (AGM) be used

to communicate with shareholders and seek their participation in the affairs of the company. This can take the form of a dialogue to develop mutual understanding of the organisation's objectives.

United States

In the US, expectations on the board of directors, senior management and the corporation itself are as follows:

1. Provide competent and ethical operation of the corporation on a day-to-day basis.

2. Produce long-term value for shareholders.

3. Develop and implement the corporation's strategic plans, and identify, evaluate and manage the risks inherent in the corporation's strategy.

4. Produce financial statements that fairly present the financial condition.

5. Engage an independent accounting firm to audit the financial statements.

6. Play a leadership role in shaping the governance of the corporation and the composition of the board.

7. Adopt and oversee the implementation of compensation policies aligned with the corporation's long-term strategy.

8. Engage with long-term shareholders in a meaningful way on issues and concerns that are of their widespread interest.

9. Deal with its employees, customers, suppliers and other constituencies in a fair and equitable manner and exemplify the highest standards of corporate citizenship.

There is now external scrutiny over the way companies operate and how they comply with guiding principles of corporate governance. Boards of directors and senior executives have been made accountable and responsible for their decisions and actions. In essence, corporate governance has imposed the responsibility that key decisions are in line with corporate vision, value and strategy, and systems are implemented that dictate how the organisation is directed and controlled. Under corporate governance, objectives that are pursued are in the interests of the organisation and its shareholders/ stakeholders and subjected to risk management.

Across all principles, flexibility is stressed. This is best summarised by the OECD (2004):

> *The Principles are evolutionary in nature and should be reviewed in light of significant changes in circumstances. To remain competitive in a changing world, corporations must innovate and adapt their corporate governance practices so that they can meet new demands and grasp new opportunities.*

In other words, the principles as such are not intended to be prescriptive by telling organisations exactly what constitutes good governance and how to achieve it. Rather, they provide guidelines for organisations wanting to achieve excellence in corporate governance.

Conformance and Performance

Principles of corporate governance indicate the existence of two dimensions: conformance and performance. Conformance focuses on meeting the expectations of external scrutiny through compliance with various laws and following acceptable and defensible governance standards. Performance, on the other hand, provides expectations about the achievement of corporate objectives. It is associated with strategic activities and seeks to maximise the benefits flowing to shareholders/stakeholders. While the former focuses on accountability and responsibility to demonstrate due diligence under the law, the latter has a leadership role linked to the execution of business activities and, therefore, has more of a business orientation.

The conformance dimension is about value-protecting and follows the principles of disclosure and transparency (OECD 2004), accountability (UK Financial Reporting Council 2010), financial reporting and audit (US Business Roundtable 2010) and managed risk (Australian Stock Exchange Corporate Governance Council 2010). Performance governance, on the other hand, is about value-creating, reflected in principles such as developing structures that enable the board to add value to the organisation (Australian Stock Exchange Corporate Governance Council 2010), leadership (UK Financial Reporting Council 2010) and those more specific expectations of the US Business Roundtable (2010), namely to produce long-term value for shareholders and to develop and implement the corporation's strategic plans. Both dimensions of governance feed into one another, as shown in Figure 3.1.

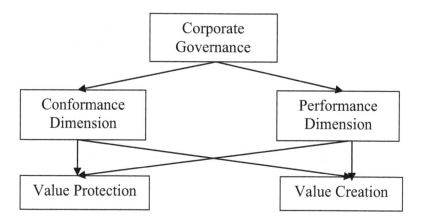

Figure 3.1   Corporate governance framework

Checklist: Compliance with Corporate Governance Principles

- Is the term 'governance' clearly understood?

- Is there an acceptance to act in the best interests of shareholders and stakeholders?

- Are the principles of corporate governance applied?

- Is an effort made to interpret them in the context of the organisation?

- Are corporate governance principles developed in a transparent manner and disclosed?

- Does the composition of the board satisfy the 'effectiveness' criteria?

- Is there a clear distinction between board responsibilities and those of the executive to run the company's business?

- Are shareholders' rights protected?

- Is there a dialogue with shareholders to achieve a mutual understanding of the organisation's objectives?

- Do all classes of shareholders have equal rights?

- Does the organisation work with stakeholders to sustain financial viability?

- Does the board provide strategic leadership?

- Does the board monitor the performance of organisational management?

- Is the board accountable for its performance to the organisation and its shareholders?

- Is the composition of the board adequate to complete its responsibilities?

- Are board members elected in a transparent and open manner?

- Are board members inducted and undergo refresher courses?

- Are board members' remuneration packages disclosed and independently approved?

- Is remuneration linked with board and individual performance?

- Is the board accountable for achieving the organisation's objectives?

- Does the board accept its responsibilities for assessing and managing enterprise risks?

- Has the board the expertise to implement enterprise-wide risk management?

- Do board members act as responsible corporate citizens?

- Does the board distinguish between its risk conformance and performance responsibilities?

Project Governance

Project governance can be regarded as a subset of corporate governance in relation to project activities; its precise scope, however, has as yet not been clearly established. According to Abu Hassim et al. (2011), project governance is a new concept and has only recently been explored by practitioners and researchers. They maintained that early studies have not provided theoretical frameworks to demonstrate the nature of project governance. Being an immature discipline requires researchers to approach the topic in a holistic manner by exploring underlying issues and developing models that are useful for practice.

One approach is to translate the generic principles of corporate governance to project governance. This would cover the expectations for conformance and performance at the project level. Senior management is used to the principle-based approach in their responsibility for corporate governance. Furthermore, principles provide the flexibility that allows them to use their judgements to design and implement effective and efficient processes and structures.

Williams et al. (2010) provided some guidance for constructing a more specific project governance framework by satisfying three main goals:

- Choose the right project. In today's turbulent environment organisations are advised to adopt a flexible, complementary and collaborative approach to project governance to gain most benefits from projects they initiate. Such an arrangement would enable organisations to realise value from projects instead of restraining their contribution by emphasising project control.

- Deliver projects efficiently. Project governance requires the alignment of project activities with organisational activities. It can therefore be viewed as a set of formal principles, structures and processes for undertaking and managing projects within the broader principles of corporate governance.

- Ensure that chosen projects can be sustained. Project governance should be perceived as an ongoing collaborative network structure between project and corporate management.

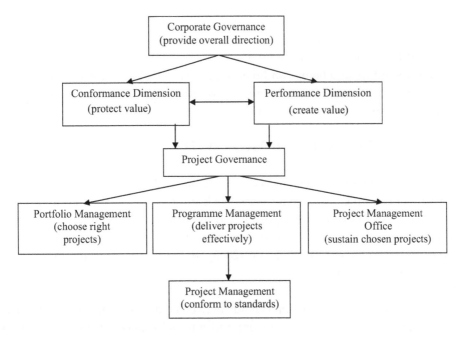

Figure 3.2   Behaviour-oriented view of project governance

In a further approach project governance is closely aligned with project management. The approach can be behaviour- or outcome-oriented (Mueller, 2009). With the former, the organisation depends on the project adhering to established guidelines and relies on the team's competency to conform to standards and policies. In addition to project management are the processes for managing the project portfolio and programmes and the Project Management Office (PMO). They have different objectives. Project portfolio management aims to choose the right projects for the organisation; project programme management seeks to deliver them effectively as a set of projects, and the PMO sustains projects by prescribing standards and best practice. These activities can be linked to the aims of corporate governance and the activities of project management as shown in Figure 3.2.

By contrast, the outcome-oriented perspective provides the project team with flexibility as long as agreed project objectives are achieved. Project management is perceived as a core competency within the organisation and project managers play a key role in project governance. According to Abu Hassim et al. (2011) the essential requirements are transparency (by providing a tangible and understandable link between what is being done, how it is being done and the project outcome), accountability (for project management) and establishing relationships (between internal and external parties). Williams et al. (2010) concurred with the criteria of transparency but defined it as being open to scrutiny and being candid about decision-making, and added learning and willingness to change. Figure 3.3 provides an overview of the outcome-oriented view of project governance.

PROJECT GOVERNANCE VERSUS PROJECT MANAGEMENT

The differentiation between project governance and management is not always clear. For example, research by Marnewick and Labuschagne (2011) found that the terms are used interchangeably. On the other hand, Sharma et al. (2009) emphasised that project governance and project management are closely related but not identical. Peterson (2003) separated the concepts in terms of their scope and focus.

Traditionally, a distinction is made between management and governance. Management focuses on the current and internal aspects of the organisation (i.e. efficiency), while governance focuses on the dual demands of future and external requirements (i.e. effectiveness). This view can be applied to projects. Project management takes a narrow perspective of managing the internal activities of a specific project at a specific moment in time. By contrast, project governance takes a broader perspective by identifying projects that best meet market needs as they arise.

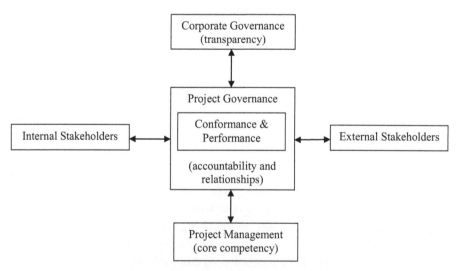

Figure 3.3   Outcome-oriented view of project governance

The primary role of project management is to deliver the objectives of the project on time and within budget as a matter of efficiency ('doing things right'). Project governance seeks to achieve organisational objectives effectively ('doing the right things') and is measured by business success criteria, such as increased profits or market share. It has evolved to a broad, strategic approach while project management has a narrow, operational approach. Project governance requires skills in organisational leadership to achieve its objectives and is carried out by executive management who report to the board of directors. Project management requires skills of a technical nature, such as project scheduling, and is carried out by middle management who report to senior management. Table 3.1 summarises the features that distinguish project management from project governance.

Table 3.1   **Distinction between project management and project governance**

Dimensions	Project Management	Project Governance
Scope	Narrow, internal, current	Broad, external, future
Primary role	Deliver project objectives efficiently	Deliver organisational objectives effectively
Outcomes	Project deliverables	Business performance
Measures	On time and budget	Business success
Focus on	Technical issues	Strategic issues
Skill required	Project management	Organisational leadership
Responsibility of	Middle management	Executive management
Responsible to	Executive management	Board of directors
Compliance with	Project management standards	Governance principles

In summary, project governance is concerned with project completion but goes beyond this by also considering overall business success. Due to its newness, organisations may find project governance to be weak but project management to be strong (Sharma et al. 2009). Project management has been practised over many years and its tools and techniques are mature. This is not the case with project governance, where processes and structures are still evolving.

Checklist: How Well Established is Project Governance?

- How well is the concept of project governance understood?

- Has the scope of project governance been determined?

- Do principles of project governance exist in written form?

- How were project governance principles developed?

- How are project governance principles disclosed?

- Do the principles of corporate governance provide guidance to project governance?

- Does project governance aim to select the 'right' projects?

- Does project governance deliver projects efficiently?

- Does project governance sustain the chosen projects?

- Do project governance activities include internal and external stakeholders?

- Is project governance distinguished from project management?

- Are the differences understood?

- Does project governance support business objectives?

Introduction to Project Risk Governance

The responsibility for risk management is explicitly acknowledged in corporate governance principles. There is a general acceptance of its importance: 'Managing risk is part of corporate governance and the ability of an entity to strategically achieve results' (Burnaby and Hass 2009: 540). The definition of enterprise governance (akin to corporate governance) provided by CIMA (2004) requires ascertaining that risks are managed appropriately. More specifically, corporate governance includes identifying, evaluating and managing the risks inherent in the corporation's strategy (US Business Roundtable 2010).

The emphasis on risk management in the context of corporate governance has elevated risk management to a strategic corporate activity. Ernst & Young (2012: 11) go so far as to conclude:

> *Risk is now becoming the fourth dimension of business. People were the first dimension. Process became the second dimension during the height of the manufacturing era. Evolving technology formed the third dimension. Embedded risk as the fourth dimension of business has the potential to fundamentally transform how organizations connect risk to reward.*

ENTERPRISE RISK MANAGEMENT

Risk management as a corporate activity is reflected in the well-known concept of Enterprise Risk Management (ERM). Taliento (2007: 255) defined ERM as

> *a process, effected by an entity's board of directors, management and other personnel, applied in strategy setting and across the enterprise, designed to identify potential events that may affect the entity, and manage risk to be within its risk appetite, to provide reasonable assurance regarding achievement of entity objectives.*

Burnaby and Hass (2009: 540) envisaged the objectives of ERM as follows: 'first, to develop strategic corporate objectives that are measurable, second, to identify risks that would prevent accomplishing the corporate objectives, and, third, to identify controls that would mitigate those risks'. Enterprise-wide risk is broadly defined by them as 'anything that gets in the way of an organisation achieving its objectives'.

Key characteristics that apply to Project Risk Governance (PRG) can be derived from the above definitions.

- Responsible parties. A clear indication is provided that the responsibility for PRG is in the hands of the board of directors, executive and senior management, and others involved in governance processes.

- Governance scope. While ERM is enterprise-wide, the scope of PRG is restricted to the processes and structures used to integrate business and project risk activities.

- Strategic objectives. PRG has an 'economic value' in that project risk is managed to protect and/or create value for the organisation.

- Risk appetite. A prerequisite for PRG is defining the organisation's appetite for taking on risks. PRG ensures that project risks stay within limits tolerated by the organisation.

- Risk assurance. Under PRG, strategies are developed to ensure that projects achieve the objective of being value-protecting or value-creating.

- Risk identification. Gaining a clear understanding of the risk concept is part of the responsibilities of PRG. The nature of project risk is strongly debated and diverse views exist about its nature, form and sources (see Chapter 7).

THE CONTEXT OF PROJECT RISK GOVERNANCE

With the increasing strategic importance of project risk, increased attention is being given to PRG. Senior management has to ensure that the organisation is capable of understanding the nature of the risk it confronts, as well as having the capability to exploit its presence. While risk management is a well-developed discipline at the project level, the same cannot be said for the project programme and portfolio levels (Sanchez et al. 2009). An effective interaction between corporate and project strategy has to take place, which in the past has proven difficult to achieve (Peltokorpi and Tsuyuki 2006).

PRG requires alignment (with business activities), integration (with project governance) and relationships (between structure and processes). This indicates a broad and holistic view of PRG where multiple governance dimensions and subdimensions work with each other. When viewed in relation to the other levels of governance (corporate and project), an overlapping scope of PRG is apparent. This is illustrated in Figure 3.4 and enables potential project activities to be strategically managed in order to gain maximum alignment between projects and organisational risk activities.

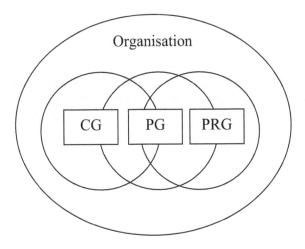

Organisation

CG   PG   PRG

CG = Corporate Governance, PG = Project Governance, PRG = Project Risk Governance

Figure 3.4   Context of project risk governance

At this stage a broad definition of PRG can be offered. Project risk governance is the deployment of organisational structures, processes and coordination mechanisms to not only minimise the uncertainties related to negative project risk but also to maximise the benefits of positive project risk. Kendrick (2004: 69) referred to this as 'an organization's ability to manage risk at both a value-creating opportunity as well as a value-protecting activity'.

Conclusion

The principles of corporate governance reviewed in this chapter provide the foundations to project governance and thereby project risk governance. Even though they originate from a diverse set of sources they have commonalities. Across principles, emphasis is placed on the responsibilities of the board of directors and the rights of shareholders. Broad guidance is provided to the board to meet its responsibilities: set the strategic direction and monitor organisational performance, engage with the shareholders/stakeholder to determine organisational goals and, importantly, implement an enterprise-wide risk management system. Project governance supports corporate governance by overseeing the activities of projects in enhancing organisational value. Project risk governance in turn satisfies the responsibility of the board to manage risks and that of project governance to add value to the organisation.

Example of Corporate and Project Governance at ABC University

The approach to corporate governance of ABC University is influenced by the voluntary 'best practice for governance' guidelines developed by government for the country's universities. Its aims are to strengthen university governance through its governing bodies, reporting and accountability, oversight and risk assessment.

The equivalent of the board of directors is the University Council. It is chaired by the chancellor who oversees the development and discussion of council agendas. Besides the responsibility to the council, the chancellor provides the visibility of the university to the wider community. He/she represents ABC University, together with other university officials, in political, cultural and economic life. Co-operation with the vice-chancellor, the chief executive officer of the university, provides the chancellor with insights into the operations of the university. However, a clear distinction is made between the strategic nature of governance at the council level and executive management of the university's operations.

The responsibilities of the council are to appoint the vice-chancellor and monitor his/her performance. It approves the strategic direction of the university and monitors the university's performance through reports submitted to it. Being a university, the performance of academic activities is of particular interest to the council. Recognition is given to the role of risk management across the university, including risks associated with commercial undertakings.

Council members are expected to act at all times in an honest, ethical and transparent manner. They can expect to be given accurate and timely information by the university's executive management and use this to make decisions that are in the best interests of the university. Their performance and effectiveness is assessed annually through a survey or through a review conducted by an outsider. Members are inducted by being informed about the council's role and the key features of the university.

Supporting the council in its governance function are the Office of Academic Governance and the Office of Governance Services. The former manages ABC University course approval processes and supports the Academic Board and its subcommittees, the Curriculum, Teaching and Learning Committee, the Research and Higher Degrees Committee and the Academic Services Committee. The Office of Governance Services oversees the university's governance framework and comprises council and committee support, university-wide records management, student complaints, and communication with the Student Guild.

A member of the council is the Director, Risk and Audit Services. This section operates in an independent manner in carrying out risk assessments and audits.

Its role is to increase the awareness of risk management, control and compliance throughout the university by conducting consultative reviews and providing client-focused advice, balanced reporting and follow-up processes. The aim of risk management is not to eliminate risk but rather to manage the risks involved in all university activities, with the overall goal of maximising opportunities and minimising adversity. Effective risk management is achieved by adopting a strategic focus, seeking to balance the cost of managing risk and the anticipated benefits of the outcome.

Project activities at ABC University are managed through the Project Management Office (PMO). It provides centralised project support, mainly for IT project delivery. Its activities are identified as:

- Providing a standardised and industry accepted method for delivering projects using the PRINCE2™ project management framework.

- Defining of project roles and responsibilities.

- Administrating and maintaining the IT project portfolio.

- Reporting to senior management on project portfolio status.

- Inducting new project managers.

- Mentoring project staff.

- Maintaining a central file storage to capture experiences in project work.

ABC University's governance activities are included in its annual report. It discloses to the public its corporate governance standards and risk management approaches and achievements. For example, it is pointed out that the risk management framework complies with ISO Standard 31000 Risk Management and that during the past year a number of risk management projects were completed. They include examining the controls of current IT systems and testing the contingency plan for one of the campuses.

Governance is an important responsibility for the university and has a high profile through the deliberations of the University Council and its subcommittees. Much attention is given to setting strategic directions, developing vision and value statements and policies and procedures. There are regular audits performed, both by the internal Risk and Audit Services, and by the external Government Audit Office. Project governance, however, has not yet been acknowledged in the university's governance responsibilities. Instead, the focus is on project management operating through the Project Management Office. Standards are maintained by following the principles of PRINCE2™.

While the positive role of risk management is acknowledged by Risk and Audit Services, there is little activity in taking on a risk-seeking characteristic. The risk appetite of ABC University is low because it is a government-controlled entity. Similarly, risk tolerance levels are restricted as public funds are at stake. However, as public funding is reduced ABC University will have to adopt some entrepreneurial activities to make up for any shortfall. It is at this stage that PRG will become an important responsibility.

4

Project Risk Governance – Processes

Introduction

Risk management at the project level is acknowledged as a mature professional activity and is well supported by material provided by various project management institutes and the well-known Project Management Body of Knowledge (PMBOK®, Project Management Institute 2008). They prescribe practices on how to effectively and efficiently identify, analyse and respond to project risk. There is, however, a lack of guidance on PRG, although its significance is increasing as organisations operate in project mode and manage project risks strategically. New processes, structures and relationships are required to integrate project risk activities with corporate risk activities. Project risk management has become a governance responsibility.

Scope of Project Risk Governance

Organisations increasingly recognise that projects deliver new capacity. From their extensive review of the literature, Sewchurran et al. (2010: 683) concluded that today's view of projects is 'concerned with managing value and benefit realisation instead of being primarily inspired by the constraints of scope, time and cost'. Aubry et al. (2007) referred to the 'economic value' of projects and identified multiple facets of this concept; a view they found was increasingly shared by several authors. They established that project management performance (time, cost, quality, etc.), project success (benefits) and corporate success (translating business into project strategy) were the key factors that add business value. Wyman (2012) provided a specific recommendation so that projects realise maximum value: he advocated linking the project's technical information with its business case.

Similarly, the approach to project risk management has changed with the emergence of PBOs. It has taken on a governance perspective since project risk plays a strategic role as outlined in previous chapters. PRG is both supported by processes, structures and relational mechanisms, and is responsible for them. Each component of PRG is discussed in the following chapters:

- Chapter 2 provides the direction for PRG from the interaction of business and project strategy. PRG aims to develop strategies that protect and create organisational value.

- Chapter 3 reviews corporate governance principles and how they are reflected in project governance. This provides an introduction to the topic of PRG.

- Chapter 4 identifies and discusses the processes required for PRG. They are portfolio, programme and project management, investment management, value realisation and performance management.

- Chapter 5 covers the structures and relationships that support PRG. They are the board of directors, project sponsors, steering committees and the Project Management Office, tied together by organisational leadership.

Figure 4.1 provides a model of PRG that captures the above arrangement. It is designed to have vertical influences of strategy formulation at the top end and those of governance processes at the bottom end. From the alignment of business and project strategy, project strategies are formulated in which project risk is avoided or mitigated to protect the organisation's value, or exploited to give it a competitive advantage. The strategies are implemented by PRG processes. They operate within governance structures and relationships as shown on the vertical axis.

Figure 4.1 diagrammatically reflects the definition of PRG developed in Chapter 2: Project Risk Governance is the deployment of organisational structures, processes and relational mechanisms that not only minimise the uncertainty associated with negative project risk, but also maximise the benefits of positive project risk.

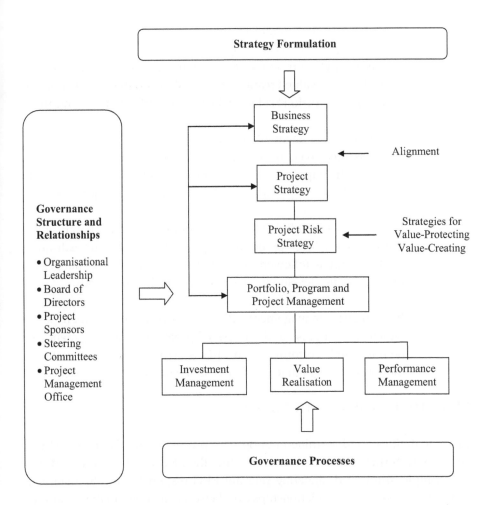

Figure 4.1   A model of project risk governance

PROCESSES

Project risk processes are generally regarded to be of a technical nature and are covered in frameworks such as PMBOK® (Project Management Institute 2008) and PRINCE2™. However, an increased emphasis on achieving positive business outcomes by projects has shifted the focus to PRG processes. They include the following:

- Project portfolio, programme and project management. The main objectives are: for portfolio management, to choose the 'right' projects for the organisation; for programme management, to deliver projects 'effectively'; and for project management, to deliver projects 'efficiently'. PRG ensures that strategies for value-protecting and value-creating are executed and that the overall risk of the project portfolio satisfies the risk appetite of the organisation.

- Investment management. Only projects aligned with strategic business objectives are considered, approved and funded. PRG mitigates the impact of negative project risk on the selected projects and exploits the opportunities offered by positive project risk.

- Value realisation. PRG delivers maximum value to the organisation during project development and implementation. A value realisation methodology is followed in which the impacts of risk changes on projects under development are continuously monitored.

- Performance management. PRG designs a set of metrics by which the progress and success of project risk management can be measured. Performance in PRG is assessed against a maturity model so that a high level of PRG sophistication can be reached.

STRUCTURES AND RELATIONSHIPS

PRG capabilities are determined not only by processes but also by structures and people. Structure can be viewed by how the PRG function is carried out; for example, through designating relevant PRG responsibilities to a steering committee. Collaborative relationships exist between members of the committee and other entities such as the Project Management Office.

- Organisational leadership. The board of directors and senior management demonstrate high levels of personal behaviour (e.g. transparency and honesty) and develop strategies for organisational success. Adopting effective communications and an overseeing role ensures that both value-protecting and value-creating project risk outcomes are achieved.

- Board of directors. Members of the board have a range of governance responsibilities as laid out in corporate governance principles. These translate to PRG and require a strong commitment to achieve outcomes that are in the best interests of shareholders/stakeholders.

- Project sponsors. The project sponsor is sometimes referred to as the project owner because he/she represents the business needs the project is designed to meet. The person often chairs steering committees and has the authority to approve or reject ongoing project funding requests.

- Project managers. They are responsible for the day-to-day management of a project and are accountable for the project's performance. The project manager 'controls' the project team and has ongoing contact with the project's external and internal stakeholders.

- Steering committees. A steering committee is set up when a project is formed to monitor the attainment of project objectives. Members are actively engaged with project activities and signal their importance to stakeholders. They remain connected with projects until their completion.

- Project Management Office. This is a central entity set up to guide and co-ordinate project work. It is generally regarded as a centre of excellence since it provides advice on project management standards and best practice.

Portfolio, Programme and Project Management

The strategic importance of managing multiple projects has sharpened the focus on the programmes and portfolios in which projects operate. Aubry et al. (2007) referred to this as 'organisational project management' in which projects are not just expected to be delivered on time and schedule but programmes and the portfolio create value for the organisation. They go so far as determining strategic alignment between them as a core function: 'the need to join together portfolios of disparate, proliferating projects into an efficient coherent whole' (p. 329). The resultant benefit of the whole exceeds the sum of the performances of the individual projects.

Mueller (2009) expressed the importance of project portfolio, programme and project management as being part of organisational governance. Project portfolio, programme and project management is tied to corporate governance through their shared goal of maximising shareholder/stakeholder value. The board of directors and senior management, when implementing corporate governance principles, are responsible for project portfolio, programme and project management. He captured this obligation as follows:

> *Governance, as it applies to portfolios, programs, projects and project management, coexists within the corporate governance framework. It comprises the value system, responsibilities, processes and policies that allow projects to achieve organizational objectives and foster implementation that is in the best interests of all stakeholders, internal and external, and the corporation itself. (p. 4)*

PROJECT PORTFOLIO MANAGEMENT

A project portfolio is a collection of project programmes that work together to meet strategic business objectives. Project portfolio management is viewed as the major interface with corporate strategy. Governance structures and relationships, covered in the following chapter, underpin the process of selecting projects for the portfolio. The governance processes of project portfolio management are shown in Figure 4.2.

Only the 'best' projects are included in the portfolio, namely those that support the interaction of business and project strategies, within the constraints of available organisational skills and resources. Mueller (2009) defined 'best' as projects of quality and short implementation and suggested that it is preferable to have a large number of good projects than a small number of excellent ones. Mueller (2009) identified three criteria by which the quality of the project portfolio can be measured.

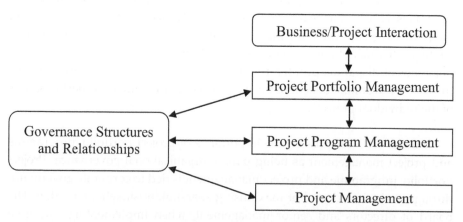

Figure 4.2   Governance processes of project portfolio management

First is the achievement of desired portfolio results. The portfolio supports the success of the business as well as its projects. For the portfolio it is about improving customer satisfaction, getting products and services onto the market in a timely fashion, increasing the organisation's financial returns, and so on. For projects, it is to meet cost, time and quality estimates when achieving these objectives.

Second is the achievement of project programme purposes. The objectives and strategies of the project portfolio are translated to the programme level and hence the same success criteria apply. Performance is measured by how well programmes in the portfolio fulfil the purposes delegated to them.

Third is to achieve strategic alignment. Each project is tested against the strategic goals of the organisation. Mueller (2009) referred to the 'strategic bucket' approach in which the project is placed under the particular strategic goal that it satisfies. The organisation would have a number of these strategic buckets. An example is grouping projects that contribute to improving customer satisfaction.

Project risks play an important part in approving or rejecting a project proposal. The financial impacts of risks on project costs and benefits have to be estimated and the project has to show a net positive return as the hurdle rate for further consideration. Alternatively, risk may be assessed in non-monetary terms when new products and service developments are proposed. Rather than focusing on a financial return, the organisation seeks strategic advantages, for example by being first to the market even at an initial cost to itself. Project risk plays an important role in investment management, outlined in a later section.

The PRG perspective is to reduce the overall risk of the project portfolio through project diversification. This requires a relatively stable environment in which long-term decisions can be made and the portfolio evolves in an orderly manner over time. With increasing volatility in the environment and the need to be responsive to new demands, this may no longer apply as much as in the past. In contemporary organisations, processes and structures are constantly being questioned and modified to adapt to the changing environment. De Reyck et al. (2005) found that fewer than 33 per cent of organisations used portfolio management to diversify and reduce overall project risks.

Checklist: Project Risk Governance in Project Portfolio Management

- Does the organisation assess the risk associated with the project portfolio?

- Is the organisation's project portfolio aligned with the PRG strategy of value-protecting?

- Is the organisation's project portfolio aligned with the PRG strategy of value-creating?

- Is the project portfolio consistent with the organisation's PRG capacity?

- Is the project portfolio prioritised, refreshed, maintained and pruned in such a way that project risk plays a strategic role in the organisation?

- Does the organisation discriminate between activities that should be managed as projects and other activities that should be managed as non-projects?

- Does the organisation engage with all stakeholders on project risks to ensure a sustainable portfolio?

PROJECT PROGRAMME MANAGEMENT

A programme is a group of related projects, managed in a co-ordinated way, superior to managing individual projects. While a project is a temporary organisation with a set of specific objectives, a programme is a more permanent structure that provides strategic direction to a project collection. Projects within the programme are related through sharing a common objective, client and/or resources, as well as through their interdependencies. The project programme achieves objectives or benefits that a single project alone cannot.

Example of a Project Programme

The NASA Apollo programme in the 1960s illustrates the concept of a project programme (Mueller, 2009). It was formed to raise the reputation and national pride of the US as a major player in space exploration. This could not be achieved through a single mission to space; rather, a series of flights took place, each representing a project. The sum of results of each project added to the value of the programme, initially in more of an intangible form (e.g. national pride) and later more tangibly (e.g. technological discoveries of the space programme could be sold to industry).

Two types of project programme exist (Mueller 2009). Temporary programmes have a defined end date and aim to achieve a specific benefit by that date. It could be a suite of computer modules within a business system, such as inventory management. Each computer module has to be designed, written, tested and implemented as a separate project within the programme of the inventory application. Only when all modules are implemented will the overall benefits of inventory management become apparent: less capital tied up in inventory holding, faster turnover of inventory items, ability to promote and increase the sale of items that provide the highest profit margins, and so on.

Semi-permanent programmes remain active as long as there is demand for the product or service. Programmes rely on the vision and entrepreneurial capacity of the organisation to continue year after year. Mueller (2009) used the example of car manufacturing. The specific model of the car continues to be made but each year it is fine-tuned by redesign or adding new features. Each change represents a project within the programme of the car's manufacturing. The programme continues until a drop in demand makes production unviable and the model of car is discontinued.

Programme management can be an alternative to portfolio management as the main interface with corporate objectives. This is seen as being realistic and pragmatic because of the closer linkage between programmes and projects. It is argued that project programmes are able to adapt better to changes in the market place compared to the larger, more inflexible project portfolio. This has particular significance for PRG since project risks are most apparent as programme/project details emerge. Compared to project portfolio management, project programme management is regarded as still being in its infancy. It lacks the current strategic approach to portfolio management, made potentially worse by the influence of heavily codified and prescriptive approaches used in the projects that constitute the programme (Young et al. 2012).

The performance of PRG should be monitored as the project programme progresses, at the end of each programme phase:

- Pre-programme. During this phase agreement is reached on the risk profile of the programme after considering the risk appetite and tolerance of the organisation.

- Programme set-up. Broad risk categories are identified within the programme and initial risk strategies determined for value-creation and value-protection.

- Programme establishment. The project manager takes on the responsibility of identifying risk at the project level and develops procedures to analyse risk, determine its significance and how to respond.

- Value realisation. During the development of projects, the impact of risks on costs and benefits is monitored. Depending on their effect, the decision is made to continue the project, modify or abandon it.

- Programme closure. A final cost/benefits statement is produced to establish whether or not the programme has produced its objective. The project team documents the lessons it learned about project risk management.

Checklist: Project Risk Governance in Project Programme Management

- Does the organisation distinguish between temporary and semi-permanent project programmes?

- Is project programme management seen as an alternative to project portfolio management?

- Is the risk profile of the project programme determined during the pre-programme stage?

- Are initial project risk strategies determined during the programme set-up stage?

- Are project risks analysed during the programme establishment stage?

- Are the impacts of project risk changes monitored during the value realisation stage?

- Are 'lessons learned' documented at programme closure?

PROJECT MANAGEMENT

The approaches to project management have variously been described as 'microscopic' and 'magic bullet type' (Young et al. 2012): microscopic, because of the narrow emphasis on meeting expectations for delivering the project on time and within budget; a magic bullet because of the assumption that following guidelines automatically produces the desired project outcome. Critics have pointed out that project managers are failing to engage adequately with top managers on the strategic aspects of projects.

Risk management at the project level currently follows the pragmatic approaches contained in guides such as PMBOK® (Project Management Institute 2008) and PRINCE2™. They provide the 'how' details to identify inputs, use tools and techniques, and produce outputs across five major stages of project risk management: planning, identification, analysis, response and monitoring. It was argued by PMI that they are 'presented as a set of procedures that are self-evidently correct' (Williams 2005, cited by Kutsch and Hall 2010: 246) and therefore have gained universal acceptance.

The foregoing discussions indicate clear differences in PRG during project, programme and portfolio management. The scope of risk management at the project levels is much narrower than during programme and portfolio management. Individual risk items are managed by the project team, while at the portfolio level an overall project risk profile is determined to meet the organisation's risk appetite. At the top level, project risk strategies are aligned with those of the business and these strategies are further developed in project programmes and implemented in projects. Different skills are required at each level, ranging from strategic to operational. Portfolio success is measured as improved business outcomes, while the project manager is concerned with the cost-effectiveness of risk management. Responsibility for portfolio management is with the board of directors, who delegate responsibilities to the steering committee and project sponsor who in turn oversees the risk management activities of the project manager. A comparison of PRG activities across projects, programme and portfolio is provided in Table 4.1.

Table 4.1   Project risk governance in portfolio, programme and project
             management

Dimensions	Project	Programme	Portfolio
Scope	Manage risk through project life cycle	Track benefits/costs in project risk strategies	Align project risk and business strategies
Primary role	Identify and respond to individual project risks	Implement value-protecting and value-creating strategies	Diversify project risks across project portfolio
Focus on	Project risk analysis and risk register	Organisational project risk issues	Strategic project risk issues
Outcomes	Project risks are controlled and monitored	Programme delivered within agreed project risk strategies	Improved business performance
Measures	Project risk response is cost-effective	Business values are created and protected	Overall business success in increased
Skill required	Project risk management	Organisational leadership	Executive leadership
Responsibility of	Project manager	Project sponsor, Project Management Office	Steering committee, Project sponsor
Responsible to	Project sponsor	Steering committee	Board of directors
Compliance with	Project risk management practices	Project risk governance principles	Project risk governance principles

Investment Management

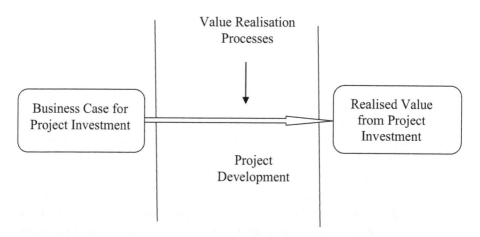

Figure 4.3   Stages in project investment management

Investment management identifies projects that meet the organisation's
strategic objectives, are cost-effective and have an acceptable risk profile.
The process is carried out in two stages: the construction of a business case

and the realisation of project benefits. A detailed business case is presented for consideration by the project sponsor to the steering committee and, once approved, it is handed to the project manager for project development. When development begins, value realisation processes provide assurance that project costs, benefits and risks materialise as estimated in the business case. Figure 4.3 provides an overview of investment management stages.

PRG plays an important role when decisions are made to invest in a project since risk and its impact are evaluated for each potential project. This requires each project to

- demonstrate that its risks are within the organisation's risk appetite and tolerance limits;

- identify value-creating and value-protecting risk strategies to enhance business success;

- construct a business case that provides a justification of the investment by identifying its costs, benefits and risk impacts;

- recommend procedures that ensure that promised values will be realised during project development and after completion.

THE BUSINESS CASE

A business case provides the best possible estimates of the costs and benefits of the proposed project and takes into account risks that could impact on those estimates. Estimates are quantified in financial terms and subjected to a cost–benefit analysis (CBA). The analysis calculates a net figure to indicate a potential positive return on the investment (benefits exceed costs) or a negative return, which could cause the business case to be rejected.

Tangible benefits within the CBA are relatively easy to quantify financially as they are mainly in the form of cost reduction. For example, the cost saving from an IT system which handles automated billing is the lower cost of the new system compared to the higher costs of the replaced billing clerks. Over time, the accounting-oriented CBA approach no longer sufficed since new benefits of an intangible nature emerged. Even though they are non-financial in nature they nevertheless contribute to the overall success of the organisation. Examples are improved customer satisfaction, better communications and decision-making quality, timely management information, and so on.

With non-financial analysis, measures are provided in the context of strategic goals and provide multiple dimensions of project value. There are a number of approaches that can be used, including the balanced scorecard (BSC) approach. This measures value along four dimensions: financial, customer, business process and learning. Each layer has specific organisation-wide strategic objectives with defined metrics to indicate how well the organisation is performing along any given dimension. The approach is 'balanced' because it requires managers to focus on more than just financial performance.

Project risk plays a significant role within the business case since it has to deal with uncertainty associated with predicted outcomes. Two main types of project risk are recognised in the business case: delivery risk and benefits risk. The former concerns the ability of the project team to deliver the project. The business case assesses the likelihood of the project being developed according to the proposed development schedule taking into account factors such as past history of on-time completions and the current level of project management skills and experience. The latter risk concerns the reliability of the estimates of costs and benefits used in the business case.

There are a number of approaches to conducting project risk analysis, as shown in Chapter 8. Among them is the 'expected monetary value analysis' in which 'best, most likely and worst case' estimates are used as determined by differences in their risk event probability and risk event consequence. The expected value or loss for each case is derived from the product of the probability and consequence; these are then compared to establish the most attractive option.

Appendix 2 provides greater detail about the construction of a business case. In summary, the information in a business case that is essential to the decision-maker is as follows: outcomes (net benefits, measurable, financial or non-financial, immediate, intermediate or ultimate), initiatives (business, processes, people, technology, organisation, projects) and assumptions (necessary conditions over which the organisation has little or no control). Since it lays out expectations of future events, the business case should be continually updated to reflect changed circumstances. It should be developed and owned by the project sponsor and key stakeholders.

Checklist: Project Risk Governance in Investment Management

- Are all project investment proposals supported by a business case?

- Are business cases reviewed for their cost-effectiveness?

- Is explicit attention given to the impact of project risk within business cases?

- Are project risks within the organisation's risk appetite and tolerance limits?

- Do business cases contain project risk strategies for value-protection and value-creation?

- Are project costs and benefits subjected to risk analysis?

- Are both tangible and intangible project benefits included in business cases?

- Are both financial and non-financial evaluation approaches used in business cases?

- Does the organisation use a template to construct business case reports?

- Are those responsible for business cases identified?

- Are business cases formally reviewed for their quality?

- Are business cases formally approved by steering committees and the board?

Value Realisation

Once the business case has received approval and project development commences, processes are put into place that ensure that costs, benefits and risks materialise as planned. These processes continue throughout the life cycle of the project to provide the project sponsor and steering committee with the assurance that the project is on track to achieve its objectives within the parameters specified in the business case. By implementing a project value realisation approach, management is able to make informed decisions about continuing to support the project, modifying the project scope, or disbanding it.

VALUE REALISATION PHASES

The concept of project value realisation can be supported by a generic approach that is well-known in IT project management. It is aptly named the Active Benefits Realisation (ABR) approach, developed by Remenyi et al. (1997) to achieve a net return from an IT project investment. Being of a generic nature, organisations can adapt its design and principles to suit their project risk management and governance activities.

ABR processes are conducted in several phases. They commence with the construction and approval of the business case before moving to the project development phase. Data is continuously collected on the costs that are being incurred, the benefits that have emerged and how project risks impacted on them. Actual data is compared to the estimates in the business case and changes to the project are considered should there be discrepancies. By a system of trade-offs between time, costs, benefits and risks, the decision is made to continue the project as is, amend the business case, terminate the project or propose a future project. The value realisation processes are evaluated jointly by the project's stakeholders, i.e. the project sponsor, project manager and steering committee. A conceptual overview of the project value realisation phases is shown in Figure 4.4.

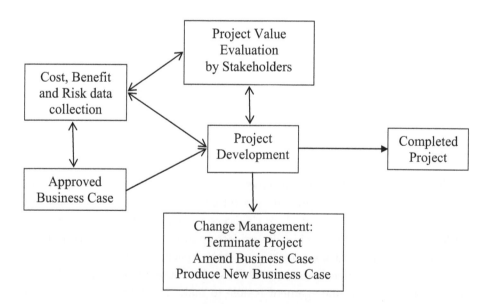

Figure 4.4   Conceptual model of project value realisation

VALUE REALISATION PRINCIPLES

ABR is guided by a number of principles which can be applied to PRG. ABR suggests the staged execution of various project processes (e.g. planning and commencement) and commitment to outcomes that will provide business benefits rather than technical solutions. PRG complies with these principles in that risk management at the project level is done in stages (planning, identification, analyses, response and control) and project risk strategies aim to achieve positive business outcomes.

The approach is comprehensive and includes the opinions of all major stakeholders. Through this, all those affected by the project are fully committed to the realisation of project benefits. PRG similarly uses a governance structure that builds relationships between members of the board and steering committee, the project sponsor and the project manager. They support the objective of PRG: to implement project risk strategies that protect and add value.

ABR is focused on a full range of benefits, both tangible and intangible. It recognises that some benefits have a direct effect on the organisation's profitability (tangible) while others have a positive effect on the business but are not able to be quantified financially (intangible). PRG applies value-creating and value-protecting strategies that have both tangible and intangible outcomes, as outlined previously.

Value realisation is most effective when it is performed regularly, preferably continuously. ABR includes summative evaluations, in which the financial impact of the new project is determined, as well as formative evaluations which are akin to learning processes. Under PRG, the organisation manages its project investments through the business case (containing 'sums' that quantify costs and benefits) and project value realisation to continuously monitor and respond to changes that occur. 'Lessons learned' captured at the completion of the project ensure that experiences are carried forward to future projects.

The objectives of value realisation are achieved through a full discussion of co-evolving requirements. ABR recommends that project benefits be realised through building relationships between stakeholders leading to a common understanding of the continuous changes that businesses and projects undergo. PRG not only applies investment management and value realisation processes, but also structures and relational mechanisms that tie together a wide range of stakeholders.

Checklist: Project Risk Governance in Project Value Delivery

- Does the organisation follow a project value realisation methodology?

- Are value realisation processes conducted in stages, viz. preparation of business case, project development and project closure?

- Are all major stakeholders involved in realising project values?

- Is the progress in value realisation continuously reviewed?

- Is data collected to provide evidence of incurred project costs and benefits and the impact of project risks?

- Are deviations from business case estimates evaluated against the criteria of costs, benefits, time and risks?

- Are decisions made to respond to deviations from estimates, viz. amend business case, terminate or disband the project?

- Do steering committees consider all requests to amend or close a project?

- Do all projects have clearly defined outcomes?

- Are completed projects reviewed for their successful outcomes, including the performance of project risk management?

Performance Management

Notwithstanding the organisation's commitment to execute value management processes, performance management ensures that project outcomes are as expected and that inadequacies in project management are promptly identified and remedied.

PERFORMANCE EVALUATION APPROACHES

Currently the pragmatic/technical approach, aligned with project management performance, appears to have a high acceptance and perceived usefulness as it is well supported by project management bodies and consultants. The approach is used by project managers to demonstrate that projects are completed on time, within budget and at a high level of quality. It is project-centric by measuring performance in project management and during project delivery processes.

The above approach has been criticised for not including an economic measure of project management performance. Aubry et al. (2007: 331) found that practitioners and researchers have not been able 'to convincingly demonstrate the economic value of investment in project management [and that] clear demonstration of the direct influence of project management on ROI [Return on Investment] is not easily accomplished'. With the economic/business value-centric approach, performance is assessed by how closely projects (planned, under development and completed) achieve organisational goals. It is directly linked to performances that improve the 'bottom line' of the organisation, either quantitatively (e.g. increased profits) or qualitatively (e.g. increased innovation).

Organisations should find a good balance between project output and project management performance, comprising technical measures and business measures. Desouza and Evaristo (2006) suggested taking a PMO-centric view. This recognises the importance of the Project Management Office (see Chapter 5) as an organisational entity responsible for the performance of project management and projects. However, they warned that performance should be interpreted within a given context which involves history and the outside. History provides insights into how the organisation is currently performing compared to how it did in the past. Information from outside indicates how the organisation is performing against organisations in the same industry or with similar projects.

PERFORMANCE METRICS

To develop metrics means applying the theory of decomposition (see Fink 2006). Broad performance measures are decomposed into lower levels until a 'succinct statement' can be made about a particular performance variable. Decomposition therefore ends at the most 'primitive' level, which is achieved when a particular performance variable has been singled out and can be measured. At this, the lowest level, the performance variable should have 'functional integrity' in the sense that the method of performance measurement is achieved through the application of a formula or algorithm. According to the theory of decomposition, the variable should make sense to those seeking to use it to evaluate performance.

Metrics provide a factual representation of important project activities and enable greater preciseness in their execution. Metrics can be used in two ways. First, they are used to assess internal performance. In this way they provide feedback on achievements, for example to determine project management efficiency, and can be the basis for strategies and actions, for example to introduce change. Second, they can be used as benchmarks from which comparisons are made with industry and other norms. Furthermore, the emergence of metrics improves the perception of greater corporate transparency.

Tried and proven approaches to justifying and measuring the payoffs of project investments in the form of traditional accounting metrics – e.g. ROI, Net Present Value (NPV), Payback Period (PP) – are popular. They have become a convenient and familiar approach for most business executives but, because of their financial nature, they tend to have a short-term focus. Non-financial business metrics have more of a long-term focus. However, to apply them, they need to be clearly understood and defined. The saying 'you cannot manage what you cannot measure' is subject to the addendum 'you cannot measure what you do not define'.

While the use of metrics can have an empowering influence, it can be threatening to some. There is now an expectation that metrics will be met. As a result, there could be a reluctance to commit to achieving targets that are perceived to be unreasonable, or a resistance-to-change attitude could develop. Undesirable behaviour may result, such as seizing control over other business activities that are not performing well or using information as a means to exert broader influence in the organisation.

PROJECT RISK GOVERNANCE AND CORPORATE PERFORMANCE MANAGEMENT

There are, however, a number of key facilitators to the acceptance of the performance metrics approach. The most significant enabler is the existing business climate, which requires today's organisation to be lean, agile and adaptive to a rapidly changing environment. Metrics track their internal as well as external effectiveness. Second, the development of cross-functional metrics, in preference to a silo approach, has increased the level of communication within business, thereby providing the environment for engaging with other projects across business disciplines. Furthermore, metrics have the potential to facilitate business integration and deliver a value framework for the organisation.

Table 4.2   **Integrated corporate/project risk governance performance framework**

Corporate Performance Management			
Demand management	Supply management	Support management	*Performance constructs*
Sales, markets	Suppliers, operations	Human resources, IT, finances, regulations	*Performance variables*
Customer satisfaction	Supplier reliability	Resource availability	*Performance metrics*
Metrics Integration			
Risk profile below risk tolerance level	Number of strategies formulated	Number of risks included in register	*Performance metrics*
Acceptable overall portfolio risk profile	Risk strategies for value-creating and value-protecting	Project risk analysis and register	*Performance variables*
Business/project integration	Investment management	Value realisation	*Performance constructs*
Project portfolio management	Project programme management	Project management	*PRG processes*
Project Risk Governance			

For PRG, an integrated corporate/project risk performance framework can be developed. Corporate Performance Management (CPM) is about 'connecting the dots' so that the various lower-level value metrics can be aggregated and made to work seamlessly together, reflecting the highest level of corporate performance. There are various organisational perspectives on what constitutes effective CPM. The Gartner Group (Koulbanis 2003) claimed that their Business Performance Framework™ holistically covers the controllable activities that occur within the typical organisation, namely demand management, supply management and support services. They are further broken down into what the Gartner Group referred to as aggregate measures, or 'performance variables', as shown in Table 4.2.

Table 4.2 consist of two parts. The top half indicates the development of corporate performance metrics in the areas of demand, supply and support management. They are termed performance constructs or broad descriptors of the areas where performance will be measured. They are initially 'decomposed' into performance variables. As an example, the construct of demand management can be perceived to consist of sales and markets. To each of the variables at least one performance metric is attached. For example, to determine the performance of sales, the metric 'customer satisfaction' was determined.

The metric is quantified by conducting a customer survey in which levels of satisfaction are indicated on a numeric rating scale.

The bottom half of the table is constructed in the same way to measure the PRG performance in project portfolio management, programme management and project management. Their performance constructs are identified and decomposed into performance variables and then 'quantified' as performance metrics as shown in the table. For example, investment management is judged by the formulation of strategies for value-protecting and value-creating for which a metric could be the number of strategies formulated.

Checklist: Project Risk Governance in Performance Management

- Are project-centric measures used to evaluate project performance?

- Are business value-centric approaches used to evaluate project performance?

- Is there a balance between project performance and project management performance?

- Is the Project Management Office involved in project performance management?

- Are performance metrics used?

- Are performance metrics understood and clearly defined?

- Does each performance metric measure only one particular aspect of project performance?

- Are both financial and non-financial performance metrics used?

- Is the use of performance metrics supported in the organisation?

- Is there a system of performance management for PRG?

- Does performance management consider PRG processes and performance constructs, variables and metrics?

- Is PRG performance integrated with corporate performance management?

Within the above framework, corporate and PRG performance are integrated at the metrics levels across the various performance constructs. It is recognised that further research is needed to increase the knowledge base of what actually takes place in practice. Baseline research should be conducted in which organisations are surveyed as to their knowledge of metrics, the perceived need for metrics and how metrics integrate. However, from the rapidly increasing interest in project performance and success, reflected in publications and conference proceedings, one can assume that the need for performance measurement is well accepted in practice.

Conclusion

This chapter defined the scope of PRG and thereby identifies its governance processes and structures. PRG processes provide the core of the interaction between corporate and project activities. They are focused on ensuring that projects achieve business outcomes and that project risk management is carried out effectively at the project level. Four PRG processes are identified: project portfolio, programme and project management; investment management; value realisation; and performance management. The objectives of PRG differ within each of the processes. For example, PRG requires risk considerations to be included in project investment decisions and during project development. The chapter concluded by recommending the use of metrics to determine performance in executing PRG processes.

5

Project Risk Governance – Structures and Relationships

Introduction

Previous chapters defined PRG as the deployment of reinforcing organisational structures and co-ordinating mechanisms by which processes are carried out to minimise the uncertainties related to negative project risk and to maximise the benefits of positive project risk. Structures are organisational entities while relationships exist between members of these entities. The board of directors is the highest authority within the structure. It is supported by steering committees and the Project Management Office. In addition, project sponsors and project managers have direct responsibilities for PRG processes by providing project funding and project development respectively.

Organisational Leadership

Leadership for governance is often found to be the factor that most separates top-performing organisations from substandard-performing organisations (Weill 2004). It should be proactive and strategic, which requires commitment and supportive behaviour from the top. Emphasis should be on transparency so that the organisation is informed how governance decisions are made.

GUIDANCE

Corporate governance principles, covered in Chapter 3, do not prescribe detailed practices of organisational leadership and hence are sufficiently flexible to be applied to various forms of governance, including PRG. This means, in general terms, that responsibilities for PRG are carried out in a clear and transparent manner so that the organisation is well aware of the strategic importance of project risk. There should be a commitment by senior management to maximise the opportunities offered by project risk for the benefit of the organisation's shareholders and stakeholders.

Active participation in PRG is required from the executive to the project management levels. The board of directors and senior managers take the lead in integrating business and project strategies and ensure that appropriate governance structures and processes are implemented. At the next level, various PRG structures develop project risk strategies as will be outlined in following sections. Leadership is about clearly setting out expectations for effective PRG at all levels within the organisation.

CAPACITY

An important leadership responsibility of the board and project management is to provide organisational capacity, defined by Henderson et al. (1996) as the human skills and capabilities required to support and shape the business. For PRG this means:

- Managing project risk as part of business strategy. PRG creates a shared understanding of business/project objectives and, more specifically, raises awareness of, and reaches agreement on, the impact that project risk has on these objectives.

- Developing strategies that distinguish between negative and positive project risk. The threats of the former are minimised while the opportunities for the latter are maximised.

- Opening channels of communication through which consensus among managers can be reached about the significance of project risks when they are identified, analysed and responded to.

- Developing an implementation plan for PRG and executing management of change processes, if required. This is about creating policy, raising awareness, delivering training and providing rewards for introducing effective PRG.

- Mentoring project sponsors, members of steering committees and project managers to create a culture that reinforces the importance of PRG and project risk management.

- Considering the organisational context by assessing existing project risk awareness, understanding and management capabilities.

By its nature the quality of organisational leadership is determined by the people dimension of governance and is therefore less formalised. When reliance is placed on humans, allowances should be made for the influence of personal traits, behaviours and motivations. The implementation of PRG may require the organisation to rethink its leadership approaches and individuals to re-learn their governance roles and relationships.

Checklist: Responsibilities of Organisational Leadership for Project Risk Governance

- Is organisational leadership aware of the strategic importance of project risk?

- Are responsibilities for PRG carried out in a clear and transparent manner?

- Are all levels of management aware of their PRG responsibilities?

- Is there awareness of managing project risk as part of business strategy?

- Are negative project risks distinguished from positive project risks?

- Is there communication and consensus about the significance of project risks?

- Are the processes and structures of PRG determined and documented?

- Has PRG been implemented?

- Are PRG activities regularly monitored?

Board of Directors

As the highest level in the organisation, the board of directors is responsible for strategy formulation, including that for projects. Business and project strategy interact to produce desired business outcomes. The board therefore has to be part of decision-making that affect projects in a number of areas. It determines the composition of the project portfolio that best meets its strategic objectives. Programmes within the portfolio are identified and projects prioritised in terms of starting and completion dates, and possibly suspensions or terminations. The board has the responsibility and authority to allocate the necessary resources to projects and thereby overcome delays that may impact delivering projects on time. It needs to develop measures that monitor the adequacy of project and project management performance.

PROJECT RISK GOVERNANCE RESPONSIBILITY

The board's responsibility towards managing enterprise risk, including project risk, is not without controversy. One belief is that risk should be managed at the operational level, below board level. It is argued that risk is a relatively simple concept to manage because 'risk is calculable, regardless of the complexities of the calculations' (Garratt 2007: 13). In other words, risk is easy to identify, define, analyse and respond to and does not require the board's consideration.

Another reason is the difficulty the board may have in dealing with external uncertainty. This requires tracking multiple scenarios in an ever-changing environment with which directors are not comfortable. Despite having to formulate policy in an uncertain world, so far '[l]ittle work has been done on the nature of directors coping with uncertainty, and yet they to continue to function' (Garratt 2007: 12). Board members are believed to rely more on gut feelings than on rigorous analysis when they decide the future direction of the organisation. As a consequence, little consideration is given to risk management at the board level; 'risk management per se is still not being embraced at board level' (Everett 2011: 5). The exceptions are organisations in highly regulated industries such as banking and telecommunications.

In contrast to the apparent 'hands-off' attitude, there is the clear responsibility for risk management laid out in corporate governance principles. The UK Code of 2010 requires the board to determine the nature and extent of the significant risks it is willing to take in achieving its strategic objectives. In Australia, the board is expected to recognise and manage risk and provide a sound system of risk oversight, management and internal control (Australian Stock Exchange Corporate Governance Council 2010). Risk management as a corporate activity is also well established in the concept of ERM as outlined in Chapter 3.

The increasing importance of projects has provided a further responsibility for the board: to balance innovation with control. PRG is at the heart of this challenge.

Project risk offers both innovation and control in the form of positive and negative risks respectively, as discussed in previous chapters. Garratt (2007: 11) believes that the role of board of directors 'is to balance and rebalance continuously their irresolvable dilemma – "how do we drive our enterprise forward while keeping it under prudent control?"'. The board has to think strategically to sustain the organisation while, at the same time, maintaining internal integrity. For PRG this requires the board to direct the formulation of project risk strategies for value-creating and value-protecting as detailed in Chapter 2.

Checklist: Responsibilities of the Board of Directors for Project Risk Governance

- Do board members have the necessary expertise to oversee the implementation of risk management activities?

- Is there a clear relationship between corporate and project strategy?

- Is the interaction between business and project strategy reflected in the composition of the project portfolio?

- Is the impact of risk on the project portfolio assessed?

- Does the board have overall responsibility for the governance of projects?

- Does the board have overall responsibility for PRG?

- Does the board distinguish between project and non-project risk activities?

- Are roles and responsibilities for PRG in the organisation clearly defined?

- Does the board have the necessary competence to direct the activities of PRG?

- Does the board receive sufficient information on significant project-related risks and their management?

- Are the board's deliberations and decisions documented and communicated?

- Are there clearly defined measures to monitor risk management performance in the project portfolio, programmes and projects?

- Does the board receive timely, relevant and reliable information which compares PRG performance against objectives?

- Is the board familiar with accepted criteria for project success, including PRG?

- Are critical success criteria used to measure project success, including PRG?

- Does the board require a PRG maturity assessment on a regular basis?

- Does the board seek independent advice on the performance of PRG from time to time?

Project Sponsors

The role of the project sponsor is essentially one of maintaining relationships with stakeholders affected by the initiation, development and completion of projects. At the highest level he/she works with the board of directors in identifying projects that support the needs of the organisation. During project development the sponsor is part of, and often chairs, the steering committee that provides oversight of the project. Close relationships are maintained with the project manager during the development of the project. Figure 5.1 diagrammatically shows these relationships.

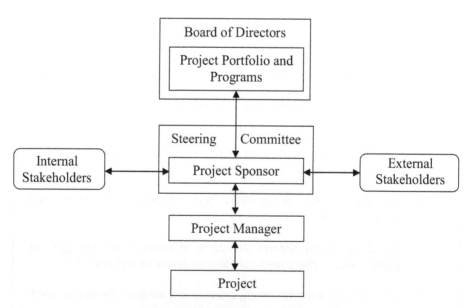

Figure 5.1   Relationships of the project sponsor

RELATIONSHIP WITH THE BOARD OF DIRECTORS

An important relationship exists with the board of directors in determining which project from the project portfolio should be approved for development. The project sponsor represents the area in the organisation most affected by the project. He or she develops the business case for the project based on his/her knowledge of project requirements. Being closely linked to the future operations of the project, the sponsor is able to conceptualise the costs, benefits and risks associated with the project investment. A budget is determined for the project and presented to the board for approval.

During project development, the sponsor oversees the value realisation processes outlined in Chapter 4. Reports are provided to the board on progress made as determined at each of the project milestone meetings. Progress is measured against the budget and project plan and funding is progressively released over the duration of the project. Should progress be judged inadequate, the sponsor may recommend that the board withhold funding and consider trade-off actions as specified in the value realisation process.

To be effective in fulfilling his/her responsibilities, the project sponsor should possess the following organisation-oriented attributes (Mueller 2009). The appointment should be at an appropriate level of seniority and be seen as one of power within the organisation. It is not usual for someone in that position not to have political knowledge of the organisation and not to possess political shrewdness. Yet there should be personal compatibility with other key players to be accepted within the ranks of senior management. Excellent communication skills are needed to articulate the connection between the project and the organisation. To see the project to its conclusion, courage may be required to battle with others in the organisation on behalf of the project.

RELATIONSHIP WITH PROJECTS

The relationship with the project manager should be carefully nurtured and professionally conducted. Among the project sponsor's responsibilities are clarifying business priorities and strategy and the decision-making framework as well as communicating business issues. This should be done in a timely manner and in a trusting relationship in which the project manager can expect to be supported in his role by the sponsor.

Being at a higher level within the organisation, the sponsor represents the interests of stakeholders affected by the project more effectively than the project manager. Hence, the role of the project sponsor counterbalances and complements the decision-making influences of the project manager. First, the project sponsor has an influence in the appointment of the project manager and that person's continuation in that role. Second, when performing the oversight function over the project team, the sponsor has the ability to challenge its conduct and performance, for example in meeting the objectives of the project. Third, a contribution to the project can be made by providing resources outside the authority of or not directly managed by the project manager.

The project sponsor also plays an important role in project activities. Most important is the ability to motivate the project team to deliver the project's vision. He/she would do so by regular contact with the team at such occasions as the project 'kick-off' meeting, at reviews and when critical milestones are reached. The team's esteem for the sponsor rises when the sponsor is willing to provide ad hoc support, as and when required. As indicated above, there is always the ability of the sponsor to provide objectivity and challenges to the project manager should it be in the best interests of the project.

PROJECT RISK GOVERNANCE RESPONSIBILITIES

The key responsibility of the project sponsor is first, to identify and support project investments in strategic areas of the organisation and second, to ensure that project managers deliver the anticipated project benefits. These objectives are not achieved without implementing effective PRG and project risk management. The sponsor is therefore an active participant in determining the overall risk profile of the project portfolio and programmes and monitoring the performance of risk identification, analysis and response at the project level.

The effectiveness of top management's support of projects has not been determined with certainty. It can be intuitively argued that senior managers play an important role in the success or failure of projects, including project risk management, but the project management literature only superficially covers this topic (Young and Jordan 2008). However, few would doubt the need for it and that it is a critical factor in project success.

Checklist: Responsibilities of Project Sponsors for Project Risk Governance

- Does every project have a project sponsor?

- Do project sponsors interact with the board to identify projects for the project portfolio?

- Do project sponsors assist in determining the risk profile of the project portfolio?

- Do project sponsors develop risk strategies for value-protecting?

- Do project sponsors develop risk strategies for value-creating?

- Do project sponsors adequately represent projects throughout the organisation?

- Do project sponsors align the interests of key stakeholders with project success?

- Do project sponsors interact with project managers on project risks during project development?

- Do project sponsors have PRG capabilities?

- Are project sponsors accountable for developing the business cases of project investments?

- Are project sponsors responsible for project value realisation processes?

- Do project sponsors report to the steering committees on the performance of PRG?

Project Managers

The role of the project manager is to develop the project according to its agreed scope. This is done by following what are regarded as logical and rational processes developed by professional project management bodies. They enable the project manager to exercise control over project activities since their prescriptive nature limits choices in achieving budget, time and scope objectives. Within a project-oriented business environment, however, projects rarely repeat themselves and are far more subject to uncertainty than previously. Being of a transient nature, but important to organisational success, Turner and Mueller (2003) referred to these projects as 'temporary organisations' in which the project manager should take on more of a 'chief executive' role, unlike the previous controlling role.

PROJECT LEADERSHIP

With an executive/leadership role, project managers give attention to the objectives and strategy of the project and how they link with those at the corporate level. Time is spent on plans and progress reports so that the project's objectives are achieved and/or plans are modified as required. Turner and Mueller (2003: 6) identified cognitive and cathectic roles. Cognitively, the project manager becomes a guider rather than a doer who should be able 'to cope with a variety of (often conflicting) goals and measures and is controlled by a board of directors and the community of stakeholder'. While responsibility was previously to a small number of people, typically the project sponsor and project client, accountability now exists on a broad scale, including to related projects and users.

Cathectically, it is necessary for the project manager to instil in the project team the belief that there is a meaningful purpose for the project. Attention is given to motivational and emotional aspects of behaviour towards achieving high-level project goals and avoiding the pursuit of sub-goals and opportunistic behaviour. There needs to be an ability to distinguish between hygiene and motivational factors (see Chapter 8). Hygiene factors are necessary conditions in performing project work such as providing satisfactory work spaces, but in themselves do not motivate people. Motivational factors, on the other hand, are important in developing superior performance and committing project members to achieving project success. They are reflected in the work itself, the level of responsibility allocated, and prospects for advancement and growth.

PROJECT RISK MANAGEMENT

To avoid the PMINO syndrome, i.e. the 'Project Manager In Name Only', Heldman (2005) identified a number of areas that require the attention of the project manager. Within them are responsibilities for project risk management.

Accountability and authority

Accountability means responsibility is taken for completing the project on time and within budget. There are tiered levels in which accountability is delegated downwards from the project manager to project team members. A project member with the expertise may be delegated the responsibility of managing project risks, or an outsider may be engaged should complexity demand this. Necessary authority is provided in the project charter. Authority is given for making project decisions, assigning tasks, choosing team members, managing performance and removing members.

Unclear expectations

Misunderstanding can arise when the project sponsor is not able or willing to communicate his/her expectations effectively to the project manager. The project manager should expect the project sponsor to be clear in the direction the project should take, to explain the relevant level of authority given to the project manager, to clear the path of obstacles that may present themselves, to secure resources and to resolve conflicts that arise. Expectations for project risk management are difficult to articulate because of the contextual influences on project risk (see Chapter 6) and the varying perceptions of what project risk is (see Chapter 7).

Uncontrolled vendors

Risk is introduced by project vendors because, as the saying goes, the vendor has the best interests of the vendor at heart. The project manager needs to ensure that vendors don't take over the project, but at the same time that vendor and project staff work together and vendor feedback is taken seriously. Vendor risk is also present in the performance of vendors when they supply the project with equipment, material and services.

Lack of project management processes

Processes are the foundation of successful projects; they provide the basis from which the project manager and team members work. There should be a deliberate conformance with approaches to identifying inputs, applying tools and techniques and developing outputs for project risk management contained in reputable sources such as PMBOK® (Project Management Institute 2008) and industry standards. Variations from these norms may cause project risk to be managed ineffectively and inefficiently.

Scope creep

The scope statement defines the project's goals, deliverables and resource requirements. Scope risk manifests itself in issues that make it difficult to meet the project's expectations. Should the goal be too ambitious in terms of deliverables and skill requirements, for instance, the risk of not meeting it or partially meeting it is a realistic possibility.

Uncontrolled changes

Project schedules lay out the tasks, responsibilities and budgets for the project. Schedule risk occurs when schedules are changed deliberately or by chance. The former requires project change management procedures to be followed, while the latter can cause unexpected disruptions to the project.

Checklist: Responsibilities of Project Managers for Project Risk Management

- Do project managers interact with project sponsors on project risk management?

- Do project managers provide effective leadership to the project team?

- Are project managers accountable for project risk management?

- Do project managers have authority over project risk activities?

- Do project managers control vendor risks?

- Do project managers follow accepted project risk management practices?

- Do project managers manage the risk of scope creep?

- Do project managers manage the risk of uncontrolled project changes?

- Are project managers familiar with accepted criteria for project success, including project risk management?

- Do project managers use key success criteria to measure project success, including project risk management?

Steering Committees

Steering committees provide a formal and effective mechanism for organisations to co-ordinate and monitor project activities. Members review and approve business/project strategy, thereby providing high-level direction and control over projects. Steering committees exist in different forms and titles because of semantic confusion about their meaning (Lechler and Cohen 2009). For example, the terms 'steering committee' and 'advisory committee' are used interchangeably (Kerr 2005), or reference is made to the 'project board' (Mueller 2009).

ENSURING PROJECT SUCCESS

Research into the responsibilities and activities of steering committees is scarce. Broadly, the steering committee is responsible for the successful development of projects. It does so by monitoring the performance of the project team in achieving project objectives within the required parameters of time, cost, quality and so on. Specifically, the committee should focus on the following activities (Lechler and Cohen 2009). First, provide a co-ordinating mechanism between the structural components of project governance. Relationships are developed between members of the steering committee representing the board of directors, project sponsors and project managers. Second, exercise oversight such as insisting on the use of acceptable standards and compliance with policies on project activities.

Research, however, has not established a link between the performance of the steering committee and value-creation in organisations. Steering committees were found to play an important role in strategic corporate planning but not in project performance or the value projects deliver (Lechler and Cohen 2009). They were unlikely to play a part in daily project decisions, although they could participate in exceptional cases. Even if they were involved, they could have a negative effect on project performance by causing project implementation delays, instigating organisational conflict or through dysfunction of the committee. The general conclusion was that 'the probability of project success or failure cannot be predicted exclusively from the presence or absence of a steering committee' (Lechler and Cohen 2009: 51).

FUNCTIONING OF THE STEERING COMMITTEE

Steering committees encompass different memberships and levels of authority and are subject to organisational culture. They are typically chaired by the project sponsor and also include the project manager. Additional members are user managers, major suppliers and stakeholders, executive management and, as required, subject matter experts. The benefit of having senior management on the committee ensures that they 'buy into' the project and thereby increase the legitimacy of the project.

Authority to make project decisions is determined by project disposition (McKeen and Guimaraes 1985). This is generally determined by the size of the project investment, and predetermined authority cut-off levels may exist. Depending on the project investment and authority level, it is the steering committee, the project sponsor or a combination of both that approves or rejects the project proposal.

Group behaviour in steering committees is complex. For instance, political preferences may override or supplement the economic rationale for investing in a project. Negotiation and bargaining take place when organisational resources are scarce. Much of the behaviour is determined by human resource management practices and influences of leadership styles and organisational culture. For more detail refer to Chapter 6.

Decisions are made on a group basis since a broad representation of project stakeholders comprises the committee. The approach differs from individual decision-making processes where the final decision is made by a person or department. Within the committee structure, reliance is placed on interpersonal communications and compromise. In the eyes of other organisational members, decisions made by the committee are often regarded with a degree of credibility and acceptability since it is assumed that the committee has acted in the best interests of the organisation.

On the other hand, the nature of projects and the composition of the project steering committee can affect the veracity of the decision reached. As a result, a portfolio with projects of a distinctive profile may result. McKeen and Guimaraes (1985) provided examples of biases towards selecting projects that support the corporate plan (which may not be up to date), large projects (they may be perceived to have a greater impact), horizontally integrated projects as they are easier to project manage (because they are within the same functional area), or those supported by formal and in-depth proposals (since they provide assurance of financial integrity).

PROJECT RISK GOVERNANCE RESPONSIBILITIES

Selecting projects for inclusion in the project portfolio and then for development is a vital function of the steering committee. How well the project portfolio and projects reflect corporate strategy depends on the efficacy of the selection process. The decision to include one project may preclude the inclusion of another, depending on the selection criteria that are applied. They should include consideration of resource requirements and, importantly for PRG, the nature of strategic risks in projects. Decision-making should be guided by sound policies and procedures, including those for recognising project risk and identifying the potential for formulating value-creating and value-protecting strategies.

By including a broad spectrum of project stakeholders, the committee is able to provide effective oversight over the execution of PRG. Members of the board and the executive are best suited to evaluate and approve the risk profile of the project portfolio and project programmes. Project sponsors and project managers have the detailed knowledge to assess the impact of project risks in business cases and during value realisation processes. As a cohort, they should develop a set of metrics by which the progress and success of PRG can be measured.

Unger et al. (2012) referred to the high-level activity of seeking strategic alignment between business and projects and the lower-level involvement in project operations as fulfilling 'broker' and 'steward' governance roles, respectively. The steering committee acts as a broker by facilitating PRG in linking projects and top management. In a steward capacity, the committee provides the resources, standards and methodologies necessary for project risk management.

As the committee gains experience with the project selection process, its positive approaches and expertise are reinforced and become institutionalised in ways that are observable. The same applies to its PRG responsibilities. Organisational learning takes place over time, enabling the committee to identify projects that are more likely to receive organisational acceptance, and to understand the factors that are critical to project success and thus avoid project failure.

Checklist: Responsibilities of Steering Committees for Project Risk Governance

- Do steering committees provide high-level direction for projects?

- Do steering committees provide high-level control over projects?

- Do steering committees provide high-level co-ordination of projects?

- Does the membership of steering committees adequately represent project stakeholders?

- Are decisions on steering committees reached by consensus?

- Do steering committees participate in selecting projects for the project portfolio?

- Do steering committees participate in determining the risk profile of the project portfolio?

- Do steering committees act as a 'broker' in facilitating the strategic role of project risks?

- Do steering committees act as a 'steward' in providing resources for managing project risks?

- Do steering committees participate in evaluating the performance of PRG?

Project Management Office

The PMO is generally regarded as the centre of excellence for project management. More mature organisations typically have a PMO at higher levels in the organisation and in centralised locations (Crawford 2006). The concept of the PMO has existed since the 1950s, but gained prominence in the 1990s because of the increasing number and complexity of projects (Aubry et al. 2007).

OBJECTIVES

There appears to be no universally accepted definition of PMOs, since they vary according to organisational characteristics and their evolution (Desouza and Evaristo 2006). However, common objectives can be identified. The PMO should take on the overall responsibility for the success of project management within the organisation. This requires the alignment of project objectives with the goals of the organisation. As a central entity, it should act independently and be provided with its own budget and resources. Staffing of the PMO should be a mix of business and technical personnel, interacting with each other. It should have the competence to develop standards and methodologies to guide the organisation's projects.

The PMO carries out specific roles and functions within the organisational context at three levels (Desouza and Evaristo 2006):

- At the strategic level. Projects that are undertaken are in line with the strategic objectives of the organisation. Business and project professionals within the PMO consider the organisation's strategic plans and use them to identify, evaluate, select and implement projects. To meet strategic objectives, projects are required to contribute to organisational growth and sustainability.

- At the tactical level. Project activities are tracked to ensure that organisational goals are met on time and within budget. The quality of project work is consistently assessed in comparison to industry standards and reputable methodologies.

- At the operational level. Best-practice project management approaches are applied during the execution of the project. Requests for increased budgets are subject to approval processes and 'lessons learned' from completed projects are made available to other projects.

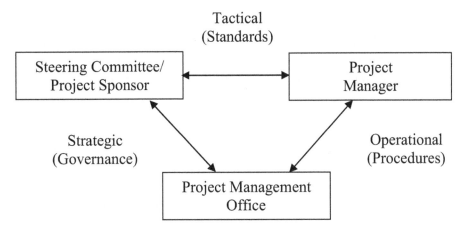

Figure 5.2   Relationships of the project management office

Figure 5.2 shows the triangular relationship between the PMO, the steering committee/project sponsor and project manager. This includes strategic governance, tactical use of standards and operational adherence to procedures.

The expectation for the PMO to play a role in value-creation was considered by Unger et al. (2012). They advocated linking the PMO with project portfolio management in an entity they termed the Project Portfolio Management Office (PPMO), a subset of the PMO. This gives increased organisational attention to the complexity of implementing strategic objectives and managing multiple sets of projects simultaneously. The PPMO was seen as improving project portfolio management quality, regarded as a predictor of project portfolio success. Its recommended structure includes a project portfolio manager, selected from the organisation's first-tier senior management, and the project portfolio steering committee.

PERSONALITIES

Caution was expressed by Aubry et al. (2010) about the ability of the PMO to contribute to organisational value due to its gaining prominence only in the 1990s and the consequent lack of clear acceptance about its role in the organisation. In particular, political influences on PMOs should be recognised since they are not outside the political system of the organisation. The researchers concluded: 'The evolution of a PMO is not always under the control of individuals who believe in PMOs' (p. 775). PMOs appear to be in transition and better understanding of their dynamic evolution is required. PMOs are best understood according to their history and within the context of their organisation.

Mueller (2009) believed that successful PMOs grow organically and that the personalities of its members evolve over time. Strong PMOs make sure that there is a balance between the three profiles. He used the metaphor of an organisational 'jungle' to identify the personalities needed for a PMO:

- The 'brown bear'. A person that has bear-like characteristics of power, capacity and intelligence is best suited at the start of the PMO. Based on their long years of experience, patience and credibility within the organisation, they can build collaborative relationships with project managers and project sponsors. The PMO gains the reputation of a trusted and supportive unit.

- The 'lions'. During the growth stages, the PMO needs a 'lion' that can roar to get his/her message across. This personality communicates PMO expectations about the use of best practice in project management. They fulfil largely a tactical function and would suit mid-career project managers assigned to the PMO for a period of two to three years.

- The 'eagles'. They hover at high altitudes and constantly monitor what happens at ground level. Within an organisational context, persons are needed that have a broad strategic view of projects, programmes and portfolio management. They are able to drill downwards to establish details should this be required. They are hard to find as they combine both breadth and depth of project management, but are required for the long-term survival of the PMO.

Checklist: Responsibilities of the Project Management Office for Project Risk Governance

- Is the PMO regarded as a centre of excellence for project management?

- Does the PMO take overall responsibility for the success of projects?

- Does the PMO act as an independent organisational entity?

- Does the PMO have a strategic role in managing project activities?

- Does the PMO have a tactical role in managing project activities?

- Does the PMO have an operational role in managing project activities?

- Does the PMO have an active relationship with steering committees, project sponsors and project managers?

- Do the personalities within the PMO complement each other's strengths?

- Does the PMO play a role in organisational value-creation?

- Does the PMO monitor the performance of project risk strategies to protect and create value?

- Is the PMO an effective change agent during the implementation of PRG?

ROLE IN PROJECT RISK GOVERNANCE

As seen above, PMOs have undergone frequent changes and are evolving to play a more important role in organisational project management (Aubry et al. 2010). To achieve the objective of becoming an organisational PMO, Bredillett (2008) suggests that the 'governance school of thought' be adopted. For this to occur, two prerequisites have to be satisfied. First, PMOs are seen as being multi-project and not single-project oriented. With the increasing number and complexity of projects, the nature of PMOs should change. The traditional approach to projects is replaced by an innovative approach, emphasising a broad range of project functions such as integrating with business strategy, knowledge sharing across projects and developing project-based human resource management. PRG is similarly a multi-faceted concept since risks in projects take on many forms. PMOs will have to adopt a dynamic and flexible approach in supporting PRG.

Second, PMOs are treated as important change agents through implementing project management methods, standards and tools. When the PMO involves itself in PRG, the organisational culture also changes: there is a move to 'projectise' the organisation and to 'buy into' the concept of PRG. Change is linked to gaining acceptance in the wider organisational and environmental context for implementing PRG processes and structures. The topic of change management is covered in Chapter 7.

Linking Project Risk Governance Structures and Processes

The PMO is a suitable vehicle to link PRG structures with processes. This is based on two premises. The PMO is perceived as a network (Aubry et al. 2007) made up of board representatives, members of the steering committee, the project sponsor and project manager. These represent different responsibilities in PRG, as outlined in earlier sections, all of which are important to the success of PRG. Although members of the PMO operate in a non-hierarchical way, they work together to implement the processes of PRG.

Second, the PMO is subject to the application of actor network theory in that it is regarded as 'a translation center' (Aubry et al. 2007: 334). It processes information from diverse projects, disseminates the information about deliverables, and facilitates debate among its members. Information about the progress of PRG is obtained from each stage in the life cycle of the project and distributed to members of the PMO. They reflect on the information received, have discussions and agree to respond to circumstances that require their attention.

The PMO is therefore ideally placed to encompass multiple perspectives on PRG depending on the objectives of actors constituting the network. For PRG, the objective is to implement project risk strategies of value-protecting and value-creating through the process of portfolio, programme and project management, investment management, value realisation and performance management. Figure 5.3 illustrates the integration of PRG structures and processes.

An alternative approach to integration is to align the responsibilities of the PMO with PRG processes for each stage in the project's life cycle. To begin, processes are applied to integrate business and project strategy and to identify projects for inclusion in the project portfolio. Members of the board and steering committee participate and approve the overall risk profile of the portfolio, taking into account the organisation's risk tolerance and appetite. When project planning commences, programme and project management processes are initiated in which project risk is detailed during the construction of the business case. Strategies are formulated for value-protecting and value-creation. These processes are managed by the steering committee, the project sponsor and project manager.

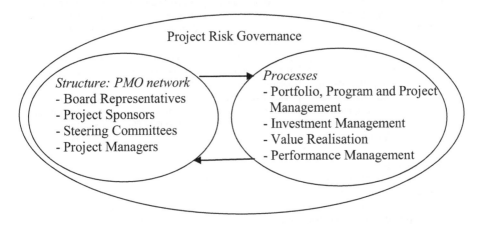

Figure 5.3   Linking project risk governance structures with processes

During project development the focus is on project management, value realisation and performance management. Detailed project risk management processes, commencing with drawing up the project risk management plan, are carried out. The main 'actor' is the project manager, with the steering committee and project sponsor exercising an overseeing role. At project closure, reviews take place to determine the business outcomes of the project investment, PRG success/failure and lessons learned that can be carried forward to future projects.

There are a number of ongoing activities that go across PRG structures and processes. They include ongoing reviews of strategies as they are implemented. PRG performance is tracked and monitored, and corrective actions are taken if necessary. The PMO continues to be the central body and adds to the excellence in PRG. Table 5.1 summarises the integration of PRG structures and processes during the project's life cycle.

Table 5.1   Project risk governance processes and structures in the project life cycle

PRG/Project Stages	Project Identification	Project Planning	Project Delivery	Project Closure
Processes	Business/Project Interaction; Project Portfolio Management.	Portfolio, Programme and Project Management; Investment Management.	Project Management; Value Realisation; Performance Management.	Performance Management.
Structures and Relationships	Board of Directors; Steering Committees.	Project Sponsors; Steering Committees; Project Managers.	Project Sponsors; Steering Committees; Project Managers.	Project Sponsors; Steering Committees; Project Managers.
Activities	Determine project risk tolerance and appetite; Identify strategic project risks; Approve overall project risk profile.	Determine project risks; Develop value-creating and value-protecting risk strategies.	Produce project risk management plan; Manage project risks through project development life cycle.	Review project investment; Review project risk outcomes; Update 'Lessons Learned' repository; Determine PRG success/failure.

Ongoing Activities
- Business and project risk strategies are reviewed and revised.
- Risk performance in portfolio, programme and project management are monitored and managed.
- Impact of risks: project costs and benefits are measured against estimates in business cases.
- PMO provides the actor network structure for project sponsors, steering committees, project managers and other stakeholders.
- PMO provides guidance on project risk management standards and best practice.
- PRG maturity is assessed against maturity model.

Aubry et al. (2007) pointed out that the PMO is essentially a fluid concept since its roles and functions remain flexible to ensure the smooth transmission of information and knowledge during the accomplishment of project goals. The manner in which processes are completed can be subjective, 'rooted in the values and preferences of stakeholders' (p. 334), and are determined by a number of factors. Among them are positions which provide or do not provide formal status, situation and authority. In addition, there are influences from the existence of knowledge and competencies, the way in which activities are accomplished, the rationality of goals (for example, integrating economic value to measure profit, project management efficiency and return on investment), an open system that measures growth and benefits, and human resource development, cohesion and morale that are almost invisible in performance evaluation.

Conclusion

This chapter identified the governance structures and relationships required to carry out the PRG processes outlined in the previous chapter. Structures operate within the broad influences of organisational leadership. The latter provides the overall capacity to design and implement PRG. Detailed responsibilities for PRG are allocated to the board, project sponsors, steering committees, project managers and the Project Management Office. While each has a specific role, they interact with each other to provide an organisational approach to PRG. The chapter concluded with a conceptual framework that links PRG processes and structures, either in a network of actors or through the project life cycle.

6

Project Risk Governance in Context

Introduction

Project risk governance does not operate in isolation but is impacted by the context in which it is applied. Contextual factors can either facilitate or impede the implementation of PRG and organisations therefore desire to maximise the former and minimise the latter. Factors are wide-ranging and can be found both externally and internally to the organisation. In this chapter they are recognised as professional associations that mentor project management practice, the principles of risk management standards, factors that determine project success, human resources management for projects, and change management. Each of them has relevance to PRG. Finally, the impact on PRG of the emerging influence of the soft paradigm in project management is recognised.

Professional Associations

Professional associations have become attractive to project managers because they reflect a degree of 'professionalism' and offer certification programmes to indicate a certain level of competence of the holder. Memberships have increased dramatically over the past two decades, with the US Project Management Institute (PMI) recording 210,000 members as at March 2006 (Morris et al. 2006).

THE PROJECT MANAGEMENT PROFESSION

A current debate is whether or not project management can be regarded as a profession, on a par, for example, with law and medicine. To form an opinion, project management's origin and traits should be examined. The practice of project management first attracted wider attention in the late 1960s when project managers met informally at conferences and seminars to exchange information on topics of mutual interest (Morris et al. 2006). This was followed in the mid 1970s by the formation of the US PMI and subsequently by the UK Academy for Project Management (APM). It can be concluded that project management lacks history in its origin, unlike law and medicine which have been practised for centuries.

A further criterion of professionalism is 'legitimacy by reference to its contribution to the public good, to an ideal of social service, or by adherence to an overarching ethical code' (Morris et al. 2006: 711). A profession should be clearly recognised as playing an important role in society and that its services are in demand. This is the case with law for those seeking to settle a dispute and medicine for those seeking a remedy for a malaise. Project management is not conducted in the public forum. It delivers projects with technical and managerial competence in a wide range of activities. Unlike the legal and medical professions, the product or service to be delivered (i.e. the project) is defined by negotiation between two parties (developer and client).

Then there is the notion of autonomy and authority. This applies only to a handful of occupations (Morris et al. 2006). An example is achieving Royal Charter status in the UK, which the APM has not but law and medicine have. The latter have stringent requirements for meeting entry standards, such as requiring a university qualification and serving a period of time under a supervising practitioner. Conditions of practice, contained in a code of conduct and enforced by a licensing body, imposed on their members are far more stringent than those of current project management associations.

Because of its business approach, project management has at times been termed a 'commercialised profession' (Morris et al. 2006). However, the development of project management Bodies of Knowledge (BOKs) is giving credibility for project management associations to act as emerging professional bodies. BOKs are developed by leading experts in the field, are open for comment and are regularly reviewed and updated. Project management can therefore be seen as evolving to a 'semi-profession' (Morris et al. 2006).

BODY OF KNOWLEDGE AND CERTIFICATION

There are three formal project management Bodies of Knowledge (Morris et al. 2006). The first was established by the American PMI in the 1980s and followed by the UK APM BOK and the Japanese ENAA (Engineering

Advanced Association of Japan) and JPMF (Japanese Project Management Forum). Coverage of project management in their BOKs has similarities, but 'the conceptual depth – the scope – of each of these three ... increases as one goes from PMI's PMBOK® Guide to APM BOK and then to the Japanese BOK, P2M. The latter two, the APM BOK and P2M, are much broader in conceptual breath and scope than the PMBOK® Guide' (Morris et al. 2006: 712).

BOKs play a significant role in the certification process since they lay out the knowledge that is required to gain recognition within the profession. Certification is keenly sought because it signifies that the holder has reached a certain status which is recognised by others in the field. It complements the shortage of alternative qualifications, in particular those awarded by universities as is the case with recognised professions. It is also seen to act as a barrier to entry and to promote the value of practising project managers to industry and commerce. While certification demonstrates that the holder has mastered the required knowledge, it does not guarantee performance in successfully completing a project.

BOKs have attracted criticism as being too mechanistic in their recommended approaches for a world where projects have a wide range of characteristics. Their apparent emphasis on control is 'more suited to achieving security of execution rather than the shaping of effective solutions' (Morris et al. 2006: 718). They provide management with possibly a false sense of confidence that following guidelines will automatically lead to project success. There are other aspects of knowledge related to professional 'doing' to be considered: know-what, know-how, know-why and care-why. 'Know-what' is knowledge acquired in classrooms about content. This is supplemented by procedural knowledge gained in practice to acquire 'know-how'. With experience, a broader understanding is gained as to the 'know-why'. Finally, the commitment to the profession brings about 'care-why' knowledge.

Morris et al. (2006: 718) summarised the current situation well:

> The challenge for the professional associations in establishing their Bodies of Knowledge is to set out the jurisdiction for project management without implying that there is 'one best way' to manage regardless of context and contingency; and to promote and disseminate this knowledge in a manner which allows intelligent and reflexive practitioners to use their professional discretion to choose how to relate to and engage the principles, concepts, models, and techniques it contains.

Relevance of Professional Associations to Project Risk Governance

Publications such as PMBOK® (Project Management Institute 2008) are attempts to codify professional knowledge about project management practice in what appears to be a logical and pragmatic manner. At the project level the logical approach, defined as 'the study of ideal method in thought and research' (Childress 1962: 321), is relevant to risk management because it lends itself to planning and control (see Chapter 8). At the governance level, the approach may be less suitable because of the diversity in which projects are integrated into business activities. This may explain why professional guidelines are lacking in their coverage of governance, including PRG.

Certificates in project risk management do not appear to require knowledge of PRG. In the APM's *Project Risk Management Single Subject Certificate Syllabus Levels 1&2 – 4th Edition*, knowledge in project management is extended to risk management. Level 2 is the advanced stage and is designed 'to allow an individual to undertake formal project risk management'. Its syllabus recognises the 'hard' and 'soft' benefits of project risk management and risk as a threat and opportunity. It also acknowledges the human factor in risk management. However, it does not address governance activities that manage project risk in a strategic manner by aligning it with corporate strategy.

Risk Management Standards

Risk management guides and standards have been developed at national (for example in Australia/New Zealand, Canada, Japan, UK) and international levels – for example through the International Organization for Standardization (ISO). The former were criticised for being too narrow by representing the views of a specific group, and lacked universal acceptance. Among the latter are ISO 31000 and COSO Enterprise Risk Management, both aiming to provide a generic approach to risk management that is recognised globally.

ISO 31000:2009

ISO 31000, *Risk Management – Principles and Guidelines*, was published in November 2009 by the International Organization for Standardization and was 'designed for a wide range of risk management practitioners, experienced or novice, and those responsible for risk management oversight interested in benchmarking their risk management organization and practices against a recognised international reference' (Dali and Lajtha 2012: 1).

As such, it supplements or replaces independent national risk management standards, such as the Australian/New Zealand AS/NZS 4360:2004, and represents a form of international consensus on risk management.

ISO 31000 is a family of standards (see Moody 2010) consisting of:

- ISO 31000 Risk Management – Principles and Guidelines. This is the primary document and provides a three-pillar architecture of principles for managing risk, framework for managing risk and process for managing risk.

  - Principles. These emphasise managing risk in business processes and in the context of creating value and making risk part of decision-making.

  - Framework. To ensure that risk management is embedded in all levels of business activity, there must be a commitment from the board and senior management to its implementation, review and continuous improvement.

  - Process. Risk is managed through communication and consultation, establishing context, risk assessment, risk treatment, and monitoring and review. The processes should be tailored and interwoven into the organisation's practices and culture.

- ISO 31010 Risk Management – Risk Assessment Techniques. This provides assistance on the selection and application of systematic techniques for risk assessment.

- ISO Guide 73 Risk Management Vocabulary. This defines generic terms to encourage mutual and consistent understanding of topics related to risk management.

Dali and Lajtha (2012) highlighted a number of positive features of ISO 31000. It should not be regarded as a standard but a guideline. The former is often associated with certification, while the latter is not. The most appropriate description of ISO 31000 is that of a 'Guidance Standard'. As a generic reference, it is not intended to be prescriptive and compliance oriented, but to encourage voluntary application. ISO 31000 'does not pretend to impose best practices but rather to harmonize principles, framework, and processes' (Dali and Lajtha 2012: 5). Within an organisation it can be a single reference point for judging existing practices and developing best practices on risk assessment and treatment. The framework provides an opportunity to integrate risk management into corporate activities, provided the approach is part of the organisational management system and not a standalone activity. Organisations should guard against 'creeping certification' when standard-setting bodies or vendors exploit ISO 31000 for commercial reasons.

Leitch (2010) offered a more critical assessment of ISO 31000 along the following lines. The terminology used is imprecise and confusing, and at times contradictory. An example is how inadequately 'risk management framework' is defined: a set of components. This is meaningless to the risk manager. Rigour appears to be lacking in that mathematical terms are avoided. Leitch (2010) referred to the absence of a definition of 'probability', a key concept that needs to be quantified when establishing the existence of risk. No advice is provided on aggregating risks. During the identification of risk and their recording in the risk register, choices exist on how they are split up. The standard gives the impression that risks are naturally occurring phenomena that define themselves. Although explicit recognition is given to managing risks from an enterprise-wide perspective, no specific guidance is provided on how this is done.

Being industry- and business-neutral, ISO 31000 is intended to have a commercial rather than a technical tone. The tension between using business language or technical jargon is demonstrated by the attitude towards compiling the risk register. Business people prefer to keep the content of the register as broad as possible, highlighting a small number of the most important risks and their potential impact on business. They prefer to gain an understanding of the overall risk environment from the identified critical risk items. Technical staff, by contrast, are tempted to go into great detail with a high level of complexity. It would be difficult to form an overall opinion on risk significance with this approach.

COSO ENTERPRISE RISK MANAGEMENT

The Committee of Sponsoring Organizations of the Treadway Commission (COSO) issued its *Enterprise Risk Management Framework* in 2004. It builds on an earlier COSO framework, released in 1994, titled *Internal Control – Integrated Framework*, by expanding on its risk assessment components (Scott 2004).

COSO identifies four categories of entity objectives and events that could be impacted by enterprise risks: strategic objectives to achieve high-level goals, the effectiveness and efficiency of the entity's operations, reporting, and compliance with applicable laws and regulations (see Scott 2004). To achieve these four objectives, COSO identifies eight components of Enterprise Risk Management (ERM). Only when all eight components are present and functioning well do they become interrelated and realise the benefits of ERM (see Hermanson 2003).

1. Internal environment. This is regarded as the foundations of ERM since it covers risk management philosophy, risk culture, board of directors, integrity and ethical values.

2. Objective setting. Establishes the targets for the four entity objectives: strategic, operations, reporting and compliance.

3. Event identification. A list of possible events that could affect the achievement of the four objectives.

4. Risk assessment. This is achieved by considering the likelihood (probability) and impact of possible events.

5. Risk response. Deciding on the strategy of responding to identified risks, viz. risk avoidance, reduction, sharing and acceptance.

6. Control activities. These are policies and procedures that ensure that risk responses are properly executed.

7. Information and communication. Strong communications and information flows to support ERM.

8. Monitoring. Ongoing activities and evaluations instead of periodic assessments.

The overall direction of COSO is reflected in its definition of ERM (Hermanson 2003: 41):

> Enterprise risk management is a process, effected by an entity's board of directors, management and other personnel, applied in strategy setting and across the enterprise, designed to identify potential events

that may affect the entity, and manage risks to be within its risk appetite, to provide reasonable assurance regarding the achievement of the entity objectives.

From the definition of ERM, Moody (2004) concluded that ERM

- is not one single action or activity, but rather a series of actions;

- processes are affected by and affect people's actions;

- allows management to consider risks in various alternative strategy settings;

- applies across the enterprise and requires a portfolio view of risks;

- considers risk appetite in pursuit of values;

- provides reasonable assurance towards achieving objectives.

Relevance of Risk Management Standards to Project Risk Governance

There are two ways of perceiving risk management standards: as a monolithic process with a set of techniques, or as a multitude of processes with a range of techniques from which organisations select those that suit them best (Leitch 2010). For early adopters, a standard such as ISO 31000 provides a good starting point for senior management taking on risk management responsibilities. They are encouraged 'to read ISO 31000, which is written in business language, in order to gain an understanding of key risk management concepts and terminology' (Everett 2011: 6). A common culture towards risk management develops within the organisation and greater certainty is obtained that risk is measured and managed consistently.

With increasing maturity, organisations realise that risk is a complex phenomenon and standards can only provide broad frameworks in which to manage risks. Standards give strong recognition to managing risks through enterprise-wide approaches and confirm that project risk processes are part of business processes at all levels. ERM is therefore a governance responsibility of boards and senior management. The standards refer to the responsibilities to provide oversight, give support from the top, assess risks relative to strategy and objectives, and establish and articulate the risk appetite. Agreement on, and compliance with, ERM is the first step to implementing PRG.

Since the release of the original ERM framework, further COSO guidelines have emerged. To assist companies, especially smaller ones, to embark on risk management initiatives with the aim of implementing ERM, COSO issued a report titled *Embracing Enterprise Risk Management: Practice Approaches for Getting Started* in 2011 (Steinberg 2011). In 2012, COSO published a new guide titled *Enterprise Risk Management for Cloud Computing* (Jaeger 2012). It leverages the principles of the ERM integrated framework to provide understanding to boards and management about the risks and opportunities of cloud computing.

Project Success

'The subject of project success is at the heart of project management' (Mueller and Jugdev 2012: 758), since the project is expected to satisfy the needs of project stakeholders, be they internal (e.g. management) or external (e.g. customers). Attempts to agree on the term 'success', however, have failed, since it is determined by whose measures one is using, what these measures are, and over what timeframe the measurements are taken (Morris 2009). Furthermore, there is a distinction between success criteria and success factors. The former are metrics, defined and monitored as part of performance management (see Chapter 4), while the latter recognise inputs to processes, structures and relationships that lead to the success of the project.

PROJECT VERSUS PROJECT MANAGEMENT SUCCESS

A distinction is made between project success and project management success. Top management is more interested in project success since a successfully completed project produces positive business results. The lack of project success is usually associated with poor understanding of customer requirements, scope creep, unrealistic planning and lack of resources to complete the project. While these appear to be obvious factors, there currently is a lack of generally accepted definitions of what constitutes project success or failure (Young and Jordan 2008).

Project management success is seen as a subset of project success (Munns and Bjeirmi 1996). Top management becomes interested in the calibre of project management when a project fails to meet budget estimates or is completed behind schedule. Not much can be done then to rectify failure, and more attention should have been given to prediction and prevention of problems that impact on project completion. A good project manager should be judged by his/her proactive (anticipating what may happen in future) and not reactive skills (looking to the past). The latter is only relevant when the project team learns from its experiences so that mistakes are not repeated in future projects.

There is some interaction between project success and project management success in providing total success. Munns and Bjeirmi (1996: 86) recognised this: 'The right project will succeed almost without the success of project management, but successful project management could enhance its success. Selecting the right project at the outset and screening out potentially unsuccessful projects, will be more important to ensuring total project success.'

Contextual factors play a large part in the diversity associated with project success. Success varies for different project types and their life cycle phases, industries, individuals and organisations, and will always be 'in the eyes of the beholder' (Mueller and Jugdev 2012: 768). New influences continue to emerge, such as the growing interest in social sustainability and business ethics. Mueller and Jugdev (2012) referred to the increasing importance of contextual factors as reflecting the multi-dimensional and networked nature of project success.

SUCCESS CONCEPT IN TRANSITION

Approaches to establishing project success have evolved over time and clear patterns can be observed from the project management literature. In the 1980s, the focus was on project implementation, then on the concepts phase and close-out phase, and '[t]oday, the success literature spans the entire product life cycle and extends from product success to business success' (Mueller and Jugdev 2012: 767). A paradigm shift regarding 'success' is occurring in which greater importance is placed on organisational than on project constructs.

Recent developments have seen a shift from measuring the success of tactical project management, with its aim of operational efficiency in time, costs and quality, to strategic project management that provides business values. The former is an efficiency measure ('doing things right') compared to the latter's effectiveness aim ('doing the right things'). Attention has moved from the success of managing individual projects to that of project portfolio and programme management. In parallel, success now includes intangible, less quantifiable outcomes (e.g. customer satisfaction) in addition to tangible, quantifiable outcomes (e.g. cost savings). The former take longer to achieve and are influenced strongly by contextual factors.

Cooke-Davis (2002) established what he termed the 'real' success factors in three areas through a survey of 70 large multi-national and national organisations. These are success in project management, the project itself and the organisation. As seen below, many of the factors reflect the orientation of this book. Project management success was identified as the traditional measure of performance against time and costs. To achieve on-time performance, the research identified a number of factors that need to be executed well. They were company-wide education about risk management, allocating ownership and responsibility for managing risk, making use of the risk register highly visible and, interestingly, keeping the project duration as short as possible, preferably below one year. To stay within the cost budget requires tight scope-change control and establishing and comparing performance against a measurement baseline.

Project success was measured against the overall performance of the project. The critical success factors were the project management success factors outlined above, with an additional one. This is the use of a project benefit delivery management process in which both project management staff and organisational management participate to ensure that project benefits are realised. The third major area, corporate success, was measured against the overall performance of the organisation arising from the completion of projects. Three factors were identified. First, portfolio and programme management practices that ensure that projects are aligned with corporate strategy and satisfy business objectives. Second, the use of metrics to provide effective feedback on project performance so that the project portfolio and programme can be realigned, if necessary. Third, seeking continuous improvement in project management through 'learning from experience', incorporating both explicit and tacit knowledge.

Relevance of Project Success to Project Risk Governance

Project results continue to disappoint stakeholders (Cooke-Davies 2002) and hence management demands to know where to put their energies and resources to maximise the chances of project success and avoid failure. Project success factors do not appear to include performance in PRG, but include aspects of project risk management. As project success is increasingly determined by its contribution to business value, a shift occurs towards project governance through the involvement of the Project Management Office, project sponsors, steering committees and programme/portfolio management (Mueller and Jugdev 2012). A similar development is predicted for PRG. An important element of project success will be the effectiveness of PRG implementation.

Human Resources Management

It is somewhat surprising that Human Resources Management (HRM) knowledge for project management is rather elementary, in that project management guidelines deal inadequately with the topic. They refer project managers to external HRM literature (Pollack 2007). Yet the 'people' aspect is present in all project activities; it is the human component that completes projects and not the processes and structures as they exist on paper.

TEAM DYNAMICS

In line with the current functionalistic approach to project management, centralised control over team members tends to dominate team dynamics. The project manager is perceived to be an expert in project management and knows best how to respond to crises (Pollack 2007). The particular characteristics of project-oriented organisations, however, have created specific challenges for HRM practices, and new approaches are required (Huemann et al. 2007; Bredillet 2008). The nature of HRM within the operations of project-based organisations can be identified as follows:

- A strong project management culture, but weak HRM culture. People in project teams often work in stressful situations because of the expectations to complete the project as soon as possible in order to gain the promised benefits as early as possible.

- Recognition of the temporary nature of projects. By definition, every project is unique, with differences in duration, scope and complexity, and requires a human resources configuration that suits it. People on projects experience uncertainty about the continuation of their position from project to project. This causes stress about two possibilities: reassignment to a new project or release from the organisation itself.

- The dynamic nature of projects. The nature of projects is constantly changing in terms of their scope, size and position vis-à-vis other projects. Employees are expected to be multi-skilled, adaptive and flexible without necessarily receiving the guarantee of permanent employment.

- A changing external environment. Projects exist in the broader world, influenced by factors such as globalisation, diversity of the workforce, expectations to share knowledge, and networking with current or potential partners.

• The need to interact with higher levels of management. Projects are vertically integrated for strategic reasons through governance processes and structures. HRM activities need refinement to provide support to governance.

Among the changes required is altering the mindset of project managers from exercising control to one that welcomes suggestions from the team. The project would co-evolve through participation of the project team and other stakeholders. Instead of emphasising being the leader of the project, the project manager becomes its facilitator and draws on the strengths inherent in the team. Team learning replaces management control. Greater collaboration is sought with other levels of organisational management to overcome project-versus-management barriers and distinctions.

KNOWLEDGE SHARING

Efforts to increase knowledge sharing among project members can readily be justified. Ignorance of each other's project knowledge or superficial knowledge transfer causes opportunities to be missed or to be under-exploited. Gaining insight into team members' knowledge and attitudes leads to better project management decisions and to colleagues' better understanding of each other's behaviour. This leads to improved reciprocal working relationships.

Accepting that knowledge sharing is desirable, the previous 'essentialist' attitude to project members changes to one that empowers them. Under the former, project members are seen to be passive and unwilling to participate in leading the team, and have a strong, insular relationship with their particular area of expertise. The latter encourages team members to share knowledge with stakeholders of the project and their colleagues. The right culture has to exist, which, according to Trowler (1997: 301), has 'moved from a position of seeing culture as *enacted* to a view of culture as at least partially *constructed* by social actors'. In other words, today's project members play an important role in shaping the knowledge culture and influence its manifestations through the attitudes they display.

The concept of knowledge is a sophisticated one, as there are many manifestations. Most commonly, knowledge is classified as tacit and explicit.

Tacit knowledge is a highly personal, subjective form of knowledge that is usually informal and can be inferred from the statements of others; it is personal, context-specific and therefore hard to formalise and communicate (Nonaka and Takeuchi 1995). Explicit knowledge, by contrast, can be expressed in print or through electronic media, transmitted through formal channels, stored and shared between individuals and groups of people through networks such as the internet, an intranet or extranet (Alavi and Leidner 2001).

Examples of knowledge sharing are easy to find in project work. A member who has participated in numerous projects would have accumulated tacit knowledge on 'what works and what does not'. When starting on a new project, he/she will transfer this form of tacit knowledge, person-to-person. By contrast, explicit knowledge, contained in supporting project material and notes, is tangible and suits itself to documentary storage and transfer. Neither tacit nor explicit forms of knowledge exist or operate independently when project knowledge is transferred. They are mutually dependent and work side by side, reinforcing the generation of new knowledge for the recipient.

The clearest evidence of current knowledge sharing is during the 'lessons learned' phase. Experiences of the project team are established, recorded, and recommendations are made for future projects. This repository is examined by the project auditor as it provides information about the conduct of the project. The auditor examines the adequacy of the policies and procedures to ensure that improvements are made for subsequent projects. Activities should take place soon after the project is closed and involve all team members, managers and stakeholders. Insights are provided into what went right and what went wrong. The following are examples of 'lessons learned' from completed projects (Barkley 2004):

- Examples of 'What Went Right':

  ○ Little or no scope creep.

  ○ Resources to resolve problems were allocated quickly.

  ○ Contingency plan was in place when required.

  ○ Communications within team was good.

- ○   Team was highly proficient, professionally and technically.

- ○   Project manager was flexible in responding to team issues.

• Examples of 'What Went Wrong':

- ○   Project changes created resources issues.

- ○   Project staff were not always trained.

- ○   Ineffective version control of documents.

- ○   Stress created by long working hours.

- ○   Schedules were not accurate.

- ○   Team sometimes did not understand the 'big picture'.

Relevance of Human Resource Management to Project Risk Governance

The performance of PRG depends largely on the manner in which organisational members accept their roles and carry out their responsibilities. Currently, HRM knowledge for project management is lacking, and non-existent for the more specialised PRG domain. Those responsible for PRG need to recognise the unique nature of projects since their impermanence determines the team dynamics. Uncertainty about tenure and career prospects may affect attitudes and motivations towards project activities, including risk management. The willingness to share knowledge among team members determines how effectively and efficiently project risks are identified, analysed and responded to. Project managers have to become more of a facilitator than a controller in the way they lead their teams. At the organisational level, senior management will have to align their approach to PRG with the dynamic project risk environment.

Change Management

Change management operates at two levels: within the organisation and within the project. For the former, the challenge is to gain acceptance in the wider organisational and environmental context for implementing PRG processes and structures. At the project level, change is usually associated with a variation in project scope which impacts project activities, including project risk management. Both require careful management of the attitudes of the personnel involved.

WITHIN THE ORGANISATION

There are a number of models that provide guidance to effect organisational change. Among the well-known are the following (see Gareis 2010):

- Levy and Merry (1986). A distinction is made between '1st order change' and '2nd order change'. With the former, changes are implemented within the organisation's existing paradigm and hence are rarely noticeable. Changes in the latter result in a paradigmatic shift and bring about 'discontinuous, deep structural and cultural change' (Gareis 2010: 315).

- Heitger and Doujak (2008). A two-dimensional matrix is used to manage change. The vertical axis shows the demands for change while the horizontal axis indicates the potential to change according to change types such as survival, repositioning, renewal and learning.

- Lewin (1947). A three-phase model changes the current state of stability to a new state of stability. The transformation is achieved through procedures of unfreezing, moving and refreezing the organisation. It requires drivers to initiate and complete the necessary changes.

- Kotter (1996). Attention is given to overcoming resistance to change and providing effective leadership. Change is managed by addressing issues such as urgency, vision and strategy development, communications, empowerment and anchoring new approaches.

- Gareis (2010) commented on the practicality of using the above models: they are quite general and vague on how change occurs or is implemented. Renn (2010) focused on psychological factors that influence the acceptance of change. He identified five factors that he found 'almost intuitively plausible' (p. 231); even more so when considered in the context of introducing governance as shown below.

- Attractiveness of information source. This is heightened when there is close similarity between the viewpoints of the source and receiver. For example, governance is achieved when employees understand its benefits as a result of completing an awareness and education programme.

- Sympathy or empathy of the receiver for the source. The receiver identifies with the source or its motivation. This could occur when the organisation is performing poorly and the introduction of better governance will lead to improvement.

- Credibility of the source. Perceived as competence, expertise, objectivity and impartiality. A 'change co-ordinator' (Stare 2010) may be appointed who meticulously and impartially documents a change agenda and drives progress.

- Suspicion of an honest motive. Receivers do not detect any hidden agenda or motives. Principles of governance are clearly articulated and decisions are justified and made transparent.

- High social status or power of the source. Determined by the relative positions of the source and recipient. Governance is initiated at the highest level and guided by various authorities in the organisation. This gives credibility that governance is achieved through consensus in the organisation's best interests.

Mueller (2009) suggested applying institutional theory to give legitimacy to governance. 'Legitimacy aims to ensure that actions carried out and decisions taken during governance are performed in way that achieves legitimacy within its context.' Legitimacy itself 'is a generalized perception or assumptions that the actions of an entity are desirable, proper, or appropriate within some socially constructed system of norms, values, beliefs, and definitions' (p. 88). There are three forms of legitimacy that can affect an organisation. Under pragmatic legitimacy, governance is justified on the basis of self-interest and achieving high benefits for shareholders/stakeholders. With moral legitimacy, governance supports actions that are highly ethical and fall within the broader norms of society. Finally, cognitive legitimacy assumes that governance is understood within the organisation because its actions are predictable, meaningful and self-evident.

According to Mueller (2009), an organisation will act and make decisions about governance that balance benefits maximisation (pragmatic legitimacy), moral appropriateness (moral legitimacy) and ease of understanding in the wider organisational context (cognitive legitimacy). Some organisations show a greater propensity towards one or other form. For example, technology companies tend to emphasise pragmatic (exploiting technology breakthroughs) and moral (improving quality of life through technology) legitimacy.

WITHIN PROJECTS

Stare (2010: 195) lamented the absence of current information and knowledge about the topic of project change management: 'Despite the awareness that changes are an important factor in the efficient execution of projects, an examination of the literature shows that the area of change management is poorly addressed.' Change can be brought about deliberately or by chance. With the former, change is usually linked to variations in project scope (Gareis 2010). It introduces risks and the need for scope control, i.e. can the project's objectives and other parameters be managed within the new risk environment? If not recognised in a timely manner, risks will have a negative impact on the project schedule, costs, quality and so on.

When a request for change is initiated, a formal change management process takes effect. The process itself involves generic steps starting with documenting the request, evaluating it, gaining approval and implementing the change (Stare 2010). How effective change procedures are can be determined by a project audit. The auditor is seen as 'another' project manager since he/she independently gathers information about the project, reviews progress against goals and develops best-practice criteria. The focus of the audit is on project management effectiveness and efficiency. Its main focus is on the project scope statement to establish how the project has met the objectives as laid out in the statement and how changes have been managed. The following are examples of topics and questions for a project audit:

- Business planning: were project risks identified?

- Organisation-wide culture: did top management provide support to project risk management?

- Project team: did they perform the role of 'risk managers'?

- Project risk identification, assessment and response: was there a systematic process?

- Key project risk processes, decisions and milestones: was there quality assurance and control and were decisions implemented?

- Resources: any constraints and how were they managed?

- Safety and reliability: were safety tests in place and executed?

- Project scheduling: were they adjusted for risks?

- Project monitoring: were risks mitigated and reduced?

Relevance of Change Management to Project Risk Governance

The introduction of PRG requires a formal change management system to be established and implemented at the organisational level. This may require organisations to rethink their governance structures and individuals to re-learn their roles and relationships. When senior management involves itself in project risk decision-making, the organisational culture also changes. They 'buy into' the concept of, and commit to, PRG. As a prerequisite, senior management should demonstrate their understanding and be able to accurately describe their governance approach. This becomes an important predictor of PRG performance.

When change is imposed at the project level it introduces new risks. If not recognised in a timely manner, they will lead to negative impacts on the project schedule, costs, quality and so on. The key challenge for project managers is to identify these risks as part of ongoing risk control and monitoring procedures and to respond in a cost-effective manner. Barkley (2004) provides an interesting perspective of how project risk management is changing. Project risk planning (i.e. planning project by project) is moving towards preparing the organisation towards adopting a risk attitude to everything that is being done, on a continuous basis.

Paradigmatic Influences

A broad definition of a paradigm is provided by Pollack (2007: 266): 'the commonly shared set of assumptions, values and concepts within a community, which constitutes a way of viewing reality'. It provides insights into the way a particular group approaches practice based on the way it determines values and evaluates the environment. Project management distinguishes between the hard and soft paradigms, with the latter receiving growing attention in the project management literature.

THE HARD PARADIGM

Many current approaches to project management follow the hard paradigm, mainly due to the way the profession has evolved. Guidelines provided by professional associations have adopted a functionalist perspective to provide clear guidance on 'how' projects should be managed. They are based on a number of assumptions. Organisational goals can be determined and decomposed into goals for each project. Management's desire for control is satisfied since quantitative metrics can be established to measure performance. The environment in which the organisation and the project operate remains relatively stable. There is a strong connection between the action of management and project outcomes.

While it is acknowledged that 'traditional PM is deeply rooted in the hard paradigm' (Pollack 2007: 272), the case is being made for the 'need to renew the formalization of our understanding of organisational project management ... [and] ... new approaches are needed in order to extricate ourselves from what looks like a dead-end' (Aubry et al. 2007: 331). Project management is a multi-disciplinary field for which multiple approaches apply, including those of the soft paradigm.

THE SOFT PARADIGM

In their groundbreaking UK research publication titled *Rethinking Project Management* and in subsequent papers, Winter et al. (2006) proposed a change in the way project management should be researched. The authors developed the following five themes. First, rethinking the life cycle model of projects and project management to one that recognises their inherent complexities. This would more closely reflect what takes place in the 'real' world. The second suggestion was to view projects as social processes with an array of agendas about relationships and practices rather than instrumental processes with their linear approaches. Projects are perceived as social interactions between people.

The focus should furthermore change from product creation to value creation. This book strongly reflects this theme since the purpose of PRG is to increase organisational value. It requires the broad rather than narrow conceptualisation of projects reflected in theme four: projects are increasingly multi-purpose in order to support the creation of innovative products and services. They have to be able to accommodate features that the market demands. The final theme is for project managers to become reflective practitioners rather than trained technicians. Rather than adhering to strict and inflexible guidelines, they are encouraged to learn and adapt their approaches to deal with complex project environments.

The above themes can be developed further into a number of distinct differences between the hard and soft paradigms of project management (Winter et al. 2006). These are summarised in Table 6.1 and illustrated in the context of PRG in the following section.

Table 6.1   Comparison of paradigmatic influences on project management

Dimensions	Hard Paradigm	Soft Paradigm
Goal-setting	Predefined	Ill-defined
Emphasis	Control	Learning
World view	Reductionist	Interpretivist
Environment	Stable	Volatile
Project management	Leading	Facilitating
Processes	Instrumental	Social
Structure	Hierarchical	Networked
Practice	Problem-solving	Problem-structuring
Values	Tangible	Intangible
Relevance	Objectivity	Contextual
Approach	Trained Technician	Reflective Practitioner
Project life cycle	Simple	Complex
Project structure	Machine-like	Living organism

Relevance of Paradigmatic Influences to Project Risk Governance

At first glance, the soft paradigm approach appears to be eminently suited to the project environment in which the 'transaction [to the project-mode] is unique, novel and transient, with high degrees of uncertainty' (Turner and Keegan 2001: 262). The hard paradigm, on the other hand, better suits the traditional organisation in which there are 'repetitive, routine transactions, undertaken by the classically managed (functional, hierarchical, line management) organization' (Turner and Keegan 2001: 262). However, this generalisation is not yet widely acknowledged in the literature because of the newness of the soft paradigm. Pollack (2007: 273) concluded: 'the influence of the soft paradigm on PM is less substantial, but it does appear that respect for this paradigm is growing within the field'.

The soft paradigm deserves serious consideration when implementing PRG.

- Goal-setting (predefined/ill-defined). In the project-oriented environment, projects with well-defined goals are replaced by ones that are 'multidisciplinary, having multiple purposes, not always pre-defined' (Winter et al. 2006: 642). Projects respond quickly and flexibly to changing markets and use the uncertainty of project risk for strategic advantages.

- Emphasis (control/learning). Too much control restricts the organisation from being an innovative one, while the purpose of PRG is to be creative in gaining competitive advantages. Organisations will get better at this as expertise is gained in exploiting the opportunities of project risks.

- World view (reductionist/interpretivist). The nature of project risk indicates that it is socially constructed through a variety of influences (see Chapter 8). Risk is not a phenomenon per se but is created and selected by humans because it is their ability to identify and respond to risk that they observe.

- Environment (stable/volatile). PBOs differ significantly from product-based organisations and are particularly well suited to respond to changing market conditions (see Chapter 1). PRG aligns itself with the more dynamic organisation structure through its strategic approach to project risk management.

- Project management (leading/facilitating). Project managers have to become more of a facilitator than a controller in the way they lead their teams. By giving attention to risk objectives and project strategies and how they link with those at the corporate level, they rely more and more on the expertise of others.

- Processes (instrumental/social). The trend is away from an engineering to a sociological approach. The linear sequence of tasks to be performed is replaced by social interactions to reach consensus on what project risk is and what the response should be. Social processes are complex because they are affected by 'an array of social agenda, practices, stakeholder relations, politics and power' (Winter et al. 2006: 642).

- Structure (hierarchical/networked). The traditional hierarchical approach to project management is replaced in PRG by a network of interactions between the board of directors, project sponsors, steering committees and project managers (see Chapter 5).

- Practice (problem-solving/problem-structuring). In today's volatile business environment, strategy is developed not only to solve identified problems but, more importantly, to identify the means to create new business value. Projects and PRG are enablers to achieving these objectives.

- Values (tangible/intangible). As tangible project benefits become harder to achieve, greater emphasis is placed on the intangible values of projects. Value-creating project risk strategies recognise this by focusing on business outcomes such as increased market share and improved customer satisfaction.

- Relevance (objectivity/contextual). The nature of project risk is highly contextual in that it is defined according to different perspectives (see Chapter 7). Perceptions of project risk are not value free, are determined by issues giving rise to risk, and take into account preferences in risk appetite and tolerance.

- Approach (trained technician/reflective practitioner). Practitioners who are trained to follow detailed procedures and techniques, prescribed by project management methods and tools, are now becoming 'reflexive practitioners who can learn, operate and adopt effectively in complex project environments, through experience, intuition and the pragmatic application of theory to practice' (Winter et al. 2006: 642). The trend is accentuated by the strategic nature of PRG.

- Project life cycle (simple/complex). The project life cycle has become less predictable, as illustrated by the SMART™ project management framework (see Chapter 2). Its ambitious aim is to achieve a balance between business issues ('what are we trying to achieve?'), technology ('how are we going to do this?') and social issues ('who is involved and whom do we affect by the changes created by this project?'). Within each question are issues related to project risk.

- Project structure (machine-like/living organism). Much of the traditional project manager's view is that of a functional and rational world, reflected in many of the current approaches to project management. However, the innovative and creative roles of projects and project risks have added to the dynamism of organisational life.

Conclusion

This chapter identified factors that can affect the implementation of PRG and therefore have to be carefully considered. Encouraging project managers and team members to join a project management association would raise 'professional' knowledge about project risk management and ensure an ongoing engagement with the discipline. Referencing industry standards is advised since they provide guidance to an enterprise-wide approach to risk management, of which PRG is part. To track how well the organisation is performing it needs to establish PRG success factors and regularly monitor their achievement. Human resource management, largely ignored in the project management literature, requires attention since it is the ability and willingness of people that determines the quality of project risk management and governance. If a culture change is required, change management processes should be implemented. Finally, the chapter identified a trend towards applying many aspects of the soft paradigm in project management to PRG.

7

The Concept of Project Risk

Introduction

Risk is inherent in all project activities and can be managed provided it is understood. The author in a survey of members of the Australian Institute of Project Managers (AIPM) found that 'understanding the risk concept' was the greatest concern to participants among the project risk management issues that they ranked (Fink 2012). The finding questioned the ability of project managers to recognise the complexity of project risk. A detailed discussion of the study and its findings is provided in Appendix 1.

What is Project Risk? – The Basics

There are many definitions of risk as it relates to projects. Among the more common perspectives is that project risk is an uncertain event or condition that, if it occurs, has a positive or negative effect on the project objective. An alternative view is that the accomplishment of a project is rarely possible without taking risks. Project risk is like exercise: no pain, no gain. Two important conclusions can be drawn from the definitions. First, risk can be any uncertainty in a project and, second, it is possible to control risk. This means that risk is integral to project planning and therefore can be managed. However, as experience has shown, not all risks can or should be managed. Project risk management should focus on high-risk, resource-consuming tasks to obtain the best cost–benefit effect.

RISK SOURCES

Risks arise from a wide variety of sources. They are both internal and external to the project and one could think of many examples. Take the risks involved when embarking on a construction project overseas. Internal risk to the project could be the lack of management experience in overseas project activities or costs increase beyond the financial capability of the firm. External risk for such a project may arise from regulatory requirements (e.g. causing lengthy approval processes) and political problems (e.g. the extent of corruption) encountered in the foreign country.

There are many factors that determine the presence of risk. The following are examples of how risk can be identified:

- By uncertainty. The term is often used interchangeably with risk, although the classic view is that they differ. This is explained in a following section.

- By insurable risk. Risks can be quantified and included in an insurance policy. The amount insured when a specified risk event or condition occurs is determined by agreement between the insurer and the insured.

- By impact on project elements. Components that are critical to the execution of the project are identified and assessed for risks. An example is if project members critical to the completion of the project because of their specialised skills suddenly depart from the project.

- By their nature. Project risks can be of a positive or negative nature, as reasoned in previous chapters.

- By their probability of occurence. The likelihood of the risk to occur can be estimated. The higher the probability, and its likely consequence, the greater the need to develop a risk response strategy.

- By the amount at stake. A cost–benefit analysis determines the nature of the risk response so that the cost of reducing or exploiting the risk does not exceed the amount to be protected or gained.

UNCERTAINTY SPECTRUM

Risk is often, and one can say usually, associated with the term uncertainty. Uncertainty can be viewed like an iceberg: much is hidden under the surface. On a continuum, uncertainty ranges from total uncertainty to total certainty. Or, differently expressed, the uncertainty spectrum ranges from 'unknown unknowns' to 'known knowns'. There is a link to the availability of information, i.e. 'no information' to 'complete information'. The scope of project risk management covers the full spectrum of uncertainty, as shown in Figure 7.1.

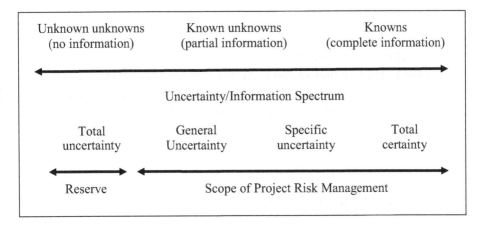

Figure 7.1   Uncertainty spectrum of project risk management

Obviously, risk is easier to identify, manage and monitor where information is complete ('known knowns') than when uncertainty is high. At the extreme end ('unknown unknowns'), it is not possible to 'manage' risk except to provide what is termed a 'reserve' to cater for risk exposure that may occur in future. It is the extent of the unknowns that represents the unseen aspect of the iceberg.

Project Risk – A Deeper Perspective

Issues in projects are numerous and interrelated and involve a high degree of subjectiveness in their evaluation. The recent global financial crisis is a good illustration of the impact of risk on these issues. Risk was present in the reckless lending behaviour in the banking sector which, when the risk was triggered, caused millions of mortgage holders to lose substantial sums of money because of the severe devaluations of their real estate. With the benefit of hindsight, many would have wished that they avoided taking out cheap but over-inflated housing loans. The loans were exceeding property valuations and causing foreclosures. The question arises: were the affected mortgage holders aware of the potential risk to their loans and, if so, what was the level of their understanding?

PHENOMENON OR SOCIALLY CONSTRUCTED?

The concept of risk is complex. In respect of its most basic form, Renn (2010) asked the question: is risk a real phenomenon or a social construction? He favours the latter by postulating the view that risk is not an observable phenomenon but originates in the human mind. Risk is created and selected by humans because of their ability to identify risk and to develop an approach to respond to the risk they observe. Ability and response, however, will vary across individuals and even cultures, depending on their perception of risk. Yet risk is integral to all our activities. The OECD refers to this as systemic risk, indicating that risk is embedded in what happens in society, business and so on. It is up to us how we react to the presence of risk; either passively or actively.

POSITIVE AND NEGATIVE PROJECT RISKS

It is usually assumed that risk has a negative connotation; it may be harmful. Negative risk involves understanding potential problems that might occur in the project and how they might impede project success. Negative risk management is like a form of insurance: it is an investment. Countermeasures are identified and funded to avoid or ameliorate such risks. In the previous example of the overseas construction project, the risk manager could have recommended hiring people with overseas project experience to overcome the risk of inexperience.

Positive risks are those that result in good things happening; also called opportunities. The goal of project risk management is to minimise potential negative risks while maximising potential positive risks. A risk strategy for the overseas construction project is to exploit the opportunity to be among the first in the market and hence be awarded further project work in future. The concept of positive risk is generally less well understood, despite the risk/return equation being well-known: the higher the risk the greater the potential return. The payback should be worth the effort and resources put into managing risk. After all, '[u]ndertaking a program is to achieve something new, to take chances, to risk' (Belev 1989: 11).

PROJECT RISKS AND BENEFITS

Barkley (2004) identified four scenarios in which the relationship of risk and benefits can be placed. For example, Scenario 2 refers to a situation of high risk but low return and is best suited for research and development projects. The opposite is true for Scenario 3, which is suitable for a project that uses proven technology in order to maximise its returns. The use of Table 7.1 supports the concept of positive risk in that it helps an organisation to identify the type of project most suitable for each type of risk/benefit.

Table 7.1   Project risk/benefit scenarios

Scenario	Project Risk	Project Benefit	Project Suitability
1	High	High	Potential positive risk with a high payoff
2	High	Low	Much uncertainty about the project payoff
3	Low	High	Opportunity to make the payoff from the project
4	Low	Low	Not worth spending resources on this project

Checklist: Understanding the Nature of Project Risk

- Is the basic definition of project risk understood, viz. an uncertain event or condition?

- Is it accepted that project risk can be controlled and managed?

- Are both internal and external sources of project risks considered?

- Is there familiarity with the many types of project risk sources?

- Is the concept of the uncertainty spectrum known?

- Is the link between uncertainty and information understood?

- Is it accepted that project risk is socially constructed?

- Is it accepted that project risk is embedded in all project activities?

- Is a distinction made between positive and negative project risk?

- Is the relationship between risk and reward understood?

- Are the different degrees of risk/reward identified?

Perceptions of Project Risk

As previously indicated, project risk is socially constructed according to a range of perceptions. Among them are those discussed below.

ISSUE-DRIVEN

Risk should not be perceived as a standalone concept but rather one that is determined by issues giving rise to risk. This can be illustrated by a metaphor. When a person decides to embark on an exercise programme, he or she will have to consider various issues, such as the level of exercise (strenuous or not), as well as possible consequences (e.g. injury caused by over-exercising) and the probability of this occurring (e.g. by considering their current level of fitness). The objective of gaining fitness is rarely possible without taking risks and being aware of issues giving rise to risk.

VALUE-LADEN

According to Thompson (2007), to determine if an event represents a risk can only be viewed as a 'value-free' technical analysis if it is conducted by a scientist isolated from the actual decision-making process. Risk is viewed as function of hazard (consequence) and exposure (probability that the event will occur) and from a rational perspective. When considering the separation of analysis and decision-making, Thompson (2007) pointed out that risk is a verb (more clearly expressed in German as *riskieren*) which is 'value-laden' because it is tied to responsible action. Hence, the person identifying the risk is also the one making decisions about it. For example, the exerciser referred to in the earlier example 'risks' getting injured by over-exercising unless he/she takes the probability and consequences of this into account when deciding on the level of exercise.

Similarly, the consequence and probability factors associated with risks are determined by humans. Renn (2010) supported this view by pointing to choices: the risk analyst has to distinguish between the possible and the chosen action and has the ability to design different futures. The way a risk event is viewed and responded to influence the estimation of consequence and probability. The conclusion is that perceptions of project risk are not value free.

CUSTOMER VIEW

Barkley's (2004) Customer-Driven Risk Management approach looks at project task accomplishment as the customer sees it. Risk is therefore associated with customer expectation, empowerment of the project team, and the effectiveness of continuous process improvement. The customer perspective is closely linked with the quality perspective in that it equates to Total Quality Management and as such would result in the reduction of risk. According to Barkley (2004), the inherent risks in a customer-driven approach are: disappointing customers, losing the commitment and support of sponsors, and users' resistance to change.

RISK EFFICIENCY

Chapman and Ward (2004: 620) focused on risk efficiency, which they defined as 'the minimum risk decision choice for a given level of expected performance'. By 'expected performance' they meant a best estimate of what should happen on average, with 'risk' being the possibility of adverse departures from expectations. To achieve risk efficiency the organisation has to change its existing practices as follows:

- From bottom-up focus on events to top-down focus on accumulated effects. Individual risks do not give sufficient insight into the significance of project risks; only when they are accumulated does the overall impact of risk on the project become clear.

- From focus on response to a specific event to a focus on collection of sources of risk. Again, a broad view on risk should be taken but this time on the sources of risks. In other words, treat the risk causes rather than their symptoms.

- From qualitative to quantitative probability impact. While qualitative approaches to risk analysis have a place (e.g. lack of data to support the quantitative approach), the quantitative approach provides more objective insights into risk. The recommended approach is to carry out a qualitative analysis first to establish the risk factors, followed by the quantitative approach to get certainty.

- From a process-based approach to an iterative approach. Risk management is similar to quality management. It has to be repeated rather than carried out once. By practising a continuous, iterative approach, project risks are reviewed, monitored and responded to.

- From constraining scope and risk to enlarging scope and risk. Organisations should not adopt a negative attitude to risk since this inhibits them and may lead to lost opportunities. The scope of the project should reflect the needs of the business, and associated risk should be accepted as being part of a project and managed accordingly.

- From focus on threats to focus on opportunities. As discussed earlier, there are negative as well as positive risks. While the focus is often on the former, the latter provide new opportunities to an organisation. The saying 'high risks – high returns' also applies to projects.

- From focus on technical fixes to focus on cultural changes. Attitude to risk, expressed as risk appetite and tolerance, is an important factor to be managed. Risk management should be pervasive in the culture of organisations.

KNOWLEDGE GAP

Regev et al. (2006) associated risk with the knowledge gap, where the gap equals what we should know to succeed less what we really know. The difference is perceived as project risk. Risk is reduced as the knowledge gap is narrowed. The topic of what is 'known' and 'unknown' about project risk is covered in the uncertainty spectrum presented earlier. Perfect knowledge results in no uncertainty and therefore a successful project. Knowledge is largely derived from past experience, which heightens the probability of achieving success.

Project Risk and Uncertainty

It is clear from the literature that not everyone has the same level of understanding about the concept of project risk. A major confusion lies in the difference in meanings of uncertainty and risk.

PROBABILITY-BASED APPROACH

Garratt (2007) provided a distinction between uncertainty and risk by referring to the presence or absence of probability. With risk, different outcomes can be estimated according to their probability. For uncertainty, the probabilities themselves are unknown. Complicating the distinction is that project risk is also associated with the risk event or condition, the trigger for the event/ condition to occur, and the estimated impact/outcome. The above conceptual complexity is illustrated in the following hypothetical example.

Checklist: Evaluating Perceptions of Project Risk

- Is it accepted that project risk is identified according to a variety of perceptions?

- Is it understood that project risk is not a standalone concept but determined by its issues?

- Is it accepted that project risk is not 'value free'?

- Is the difficulty of estimating risk probabilities and consequences understood?

- Is the customer view of project risk considered?

- Are the various project risk efficiency strategies considered?

- Is the gap narrowed between what is 'known' and 'unknown' about project risk?

Example of Project Risk Event and Characteristics

The project is the development of a new airport terminal and the key objective is to have a smooth opening day. Part of the project was the installation of an automatic baggage handling system, not used before in other airports in the region. Uncertainty therefore exists about this system. One of the risks is the event of the automatic system breaking down. The probability of this occurring is regarded as high because of the adoption of new technology, and so is the impact since baggage would quickly pile up. The risk itself is triggered by the malfunction of the new system which would result in a negative outcome because travellers would feel frustrated and avoid the airport in future. On the other hand, there could be a positive outcome should the risk event not be triggered. In this case travellers would be pleased since the tediousness of baggage handling is replaced by an automated system. Table 7.2 summarises the two scenarios and shows the different outcomes for negative and positive project risk. It also indicates that probability is not associated with uncertainty but with the risk event/condition.

Table 7.2   Risk events and associated risk characteristics

Concept	Description
Project objective	Smooth opening of airport terminal.
Uncertainty	About the automated baggage handling system.
Negative risk event/condition	Automatic baggage handling system breaks down.
Risk trigger	Malfunction of automated baggage handling system.
Probability	High – new technology.
Impact	High – baggage piling up leading to chaos.
Outcome	Value loss – travellers are frustrated by delays and boycott airport in future.
Positive risk event/condition	Automatic baggage handling system works reliably and efficiently.
Risk trigger	Automated baggage handling system operates as planned.
Outcome	Value gain – travellers are pleased by speed of baggage handling and will prefer airport to others.

CRITICISM OF PROBABILITY-BASED APPROACH

The use of 'probability' to distinguish between risk (presence of probability) and uncertainty (absence of probability) has been termed the 'classic' position and ascribed to Knight (1921, referenced in Garratt 2007). However, this position is not universally accepted. Chapman (2006) argued that the modern economist's view is to use the terms risk and uncertainty interchangeably. He dismisses the differentiation by claiming that it 'is simply a question of whether or not this is a useful thing to do' (p. 309). Management would find the task too difficult and should focus on uncertainty first, 'to define expectations' (p. 309), and then consider risks. Chapman (2006) suggested that organisations develop their own processes to managing project uncertainties and risks, based on their experience or knowledge.

Pender (2001) also challenged the underlying assumptions of the probability-based approach to project risk management by pointing out its limitations when applied in practice. He suggested that project management should have a greater awareness of the shortcomings of the theory. He identified the following assumptions and how they are ameliorated in practice:

- Probability theory is based on randomness while projects are consciously planned. There is nothing random in the way humans act and interact when following accepted best practice in developing a project.

- Statistical aggregates do not apply because each project is unique. Statistics are based on repeatable trials or experiments while the experience gained in one project cannot necessarily be repeated in subsequent projects.

- The future is fundamentally unknown and probability cannot be estimated. Uncertainty exists with projects because of variations in future outcomes for which a probability distribution cannot be constructed. Often, 'future states cannot even be imagined let alone be defined' (Pender 2001: 81).

- Human ability to deal with the probability concept is limited by their information processing capability. It is accepted that we have limited capacity to process information beyond 'seven, plus or minus two' items. Hence, '[i]t is often beyond our capacity to comprehend a complete set of future outcomes (as required by the tools of probability)' (Pender 2001: 81).

- Communication about probabilities between humans is weak because of the imprecision of our language. 'Many occurrences on a project are open to elastic interpretation and the consequence of this fuzziness can only be managed by effective and persistent communications' (Pender 2001: 84).

Besner and Hobbs (2012) examined how effectively project managers responded to project uncertainty. While their study showed that there was a positive correlation between the level of project definition and the use of project risk management practices, they argued that management of project uncertainty requires flexibility beyond the techniques that are currently practised by project teams. 'A risk is by definition a foreseeable quantifiable event, risk management is thus not well suited to the task of managing unforeseeable uncertainty, other tools or approaches are needed' (p. 242). They should provide the necessary flexibility to manage uncertainty.

Project Risk Appetite and Tolerance

Attitudes to project risk in organisations are determined in the context of the general risk environment and the objective of protecting and enhancing shareholder/stakeholder value. Choices have to be made when considerations are given to new products and/or services, how they are made and distributed and so on in what is a turbulent business environment. This is when the concepts of risk appetite and tolerance play an important role. Some use the terms interchangeably while others see clear differences as outlined below.

RISKS APPETITE

Risk appetite is the broad-based amount of risk an organisation or other entity is willing to accept in the pursuit of its mission. It is determined by two factors (ISACA 2009). First, the organisation's capacity to absorb losses such as reputation damage, and second, management's culture or predisposition towards risk taking, ranging from risk averse to risk seeking. The positive aspect of risk appetite is the amount of satisfaction or pleasure received from a potential risk payoff. This is referred to as risk utility and is linked to risk preference. Utility rises at a decreasing rate for people who are risk averse. Those who are risk seeking have a higher tolerance for risk and their satisfaction increases when more payoff is at stake. The risk-neutral approach achieves a balance between risk and payoff.

'Risk appetite is not a static concept with individuals', according to Kendrick (2004: 73). He refers to research that has shown differences in perceptions of risk and risk decision-making according to a range of factors: gender, ethnicity, risk framing, mood factors, dispersion effects, moral and ethical considerations, and experience from previous risk situations. Basic risk preferences can be observed in the way people behave in actual circumstances and assess risk severity (Schoemaker 1993). There are distinct behaviours that risk-takers exhibit: economic, decision theoretic, psychological and biological.

Under the economic perspective, risk-taking is largely determined by the shape of the relevant utility function (e.g. achieving optimal savings). Someone applying decision theory would use a rigorous methodology, while under the psychological view the risk-taker considers task, decision frames and acknowledges limitations in human information processing capabilities. A biological perspective can be observed in behaviour such as sensation seeking, impulsivity, extraversion. For example, low-sensation seekers appraise risk as more dangerous and less pleasurable than high-sensation seekers. The above diversity potentially poses problems to the risk manager not familiar with human nature. He or she may observe different manifestations to risk-taking with different project members and under different project circumstances.

RISK TOLERANCE

This can be defined as the acceptable variation relative to the achievement of an objective. It is the tolerable deviation from the level set by the risk appetite and business objective. While at lower levels different tolerance levels may apply, at the enterprise level the overall exposure must not exceed the specified risk appetite. Risk appetite and risk tolerance therefore go hand in hand and both are determined and covered by policies set by executives. ISACA (2009) warned that levels that are 'cast in stone' may inhibit the organisation in exploiting new business opportunities. Kendrick (2004) suggested that organisations should be sufficiently robust to deal with environmental fluctuations and be flexible enough to rapidly sense and respond to changes. It may, therefore, be preferable to have 'lines in the sand' as opposed to fixed limits of risk tolerance to permit a degree of agility and innovativeness.

There may, however, be situations where the organisation has no choice but to enforce a strict risk tolerance when failure to comply with specific legal requirements or regulations attract severe penalties. Each organisation will have to define its own risk appetite and tolerance levels. This ensures that there is board approval and clear communications to all stakeholders that organisational decision-making is risk based and track is kept of the overall risk profile.

APPROACHES

The approach to determining risk appetite and tolerance may well differ across the globe. Differences are due to the two main corporate governance styles (Taliento 2007). Under the Anglo-Saxon/American (including Australia) paradigm, governance is market based (believing in free competition) and shareholder oriented (maximising their return), while the Latin/German/ Japanese paradigm is credit based (influenced by lenders such as banks) and stakeholder oriented (meeting the needs of suppliers and customers). The attitude to risk management in Australia, for example, is influenced by the following characteristics: large corporations with decision power in the hands of managers, watchdog oversight over management activity by auditors and legislators, and management seeking to create value for shareholders with a habit of preferring short-term performance.

What the Australian approach appears to be lacking is the orientation of the Latin/German/Japanese paradigm, namely considering the interests of all stakeholders. This points to the need to include diverse opinions and achieve a balance between formal processes and structure and human behaviour. Renn (2010: 3) referred to this as dealing with both the physical and social dimensions of risk in order 'to avoid the naive realism of risk as a purely objective category, as well as the relativistic perspective of making all risk judgments subjective reflections of power and interests'.

Kutsch and Hall (2010: 245) saw a further problem as one of ignoring the input to risk analysis; 'the precise nature of the input does not seem to have been explored adequately in previous research'. Traditionally, risk management techniques have focused on techniques and outputs rather than inputs. The question arises to what extent inputs are identified and processed to determine risk outputs, especially when there is 'a deliberate inattention of risk actors to risk'. The authors found that deliberate ignorance of risk events by stakeholders has not attracted the attention of project managers. Attention towards the relevance of risk information may therefore be determined by organisational rather than project management culture.

Conclusion

This chapter indicated the complexity of the project risk concept. In its simplest form, project risk is uncertainty inherent in future events or conditions. These events/conditions arise from many sources and are determined by human perception. Humans in turn rely on information about the future which can range from complete, creating certainty, to incomplete, creating uncertainty. Perceptions are influences by a range of factors including how the person judges the risk/rewards equation, and vary between being issue-driven, adopting a customer view or seeking risk efficiency. The issues associated with each project risk event or condition need to be understood so that risk triggers are recognised and probabilities and consequences are determined. Finally, the organisation has to determine and publish its project risks appetite and tolerance levels to provide guidance to risk behaviour.

Checklist: Understanding the Concepts of Risk Appetite and Risk Tolerance

- Are the concepts of risk appetite and tolerance used interchangeably or separately?

- Is the definition of risk appetite known?

- Are the factors that determine risk appetite known?

- Is a distinction made between the risk utility and risk preference?

- Is it accepted that risk appetite is not static?

- Are the different attitudes to risk, ranging from risk averse to risk seeking, identified?

- Is the definition of risk tolerance known?

- Is the relationship between risk appetite and tolerance understood?

- Is there a preference for having 'lines in the sand' rather than fixed limits for risk tolerance?

- Does the corporate governance style impact on the attitude to risk appetite and tolerance?

- Does PRG consider project risk appetites and tolerances?

- Do organisational risk appetites and tolerances support the objectives of project risk value-protecting and value-creating strategies?

- Do the risk appetites and tolerances of the project team align with those of the organisation?

8

Essentials of Project Risk Management

Introduction

In Chapter 2, PRG was defined as the deployment of organisational structures, processes and coordination mechanisms to not only minimise the uncertainties related to negative project risk but also to maximise the benefits of positive project risk. Its scope overlaps with corporate and project governance to gain maximum alignment between projects and organisational risk activities. This chapter presents the processes at the project level regarded as essential to achieving the desired alignment. It begins by describing the nature of projects and the role of risk and reward in the project life cycle. Processes that are critical to effective project risk management are then identified: the project risk management plan, project risk analysis and ranking, the project risk register, implementation of risk responses, and the functioning of the project team.

Understanding Projects

In its simplest form, a project is a temporary endeavour undertaken to produce a unique product or service. It is temporary because it has a definitive beginning and end, and it is unique because a project is a new undertaking, covering unfamiliar ground. Figure 8.1 shows how these two features impact on the characteristics of a project.

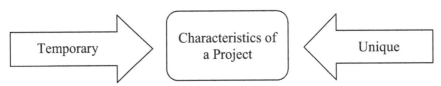

Figure 8.1   Features of projects

Example of the Characteristics of a Project

An example of a project is the university sending a team to recruit students at an offshore education trade fair. The project is temporary as it starts when the university staff leave on their travels and ends with their return. It is unique because they attend a particular trade fair, it is undertaken by a specific group of people, and it involves a travel schedule agreed for that trip. All of these elements introduce risks into the project.

PROJECT LIFE CYCLE

When the above project example is examined more closely it can be seen to evolve according to the project life cycle with the following stages (Chapman and Ward 2003).

- Conception. The project is conceived, typically by stakeholders, and the scope and objectives are broadly defined. The university decides to send a delegation to the education trade fair to exploit an opportunity to recruit overseas students into its programmes.

- Design. More details about the project are developed, including costs and benefits. They are established for various travel arrangements and the estimated number of students to be recruited. Decisions are made about the logistics of the trip.

- Plan. This includes the travel schedule, important milestones, and recruitment targets. The attendance at the education trade fair is refined with details about the number and calibre of staff travelling, and the required accommodation arrangements.

- Allocation. Resources are allocated and they include those from outside. A budget is drawn up covering registration fees, accommodation allowances and possibly a subsidy from government to promote local education on a broader scale at the fair.

- Execution. The project is carried out. The team travels overseas, registers at the fair, meets prospective students and provides them with offers to enrol in the university's programmes.

- Delivery. The product is delivered when the recruited overseas students arrive at the home campus and start their courses.

- Review. A review of the processes is carried out and the project audit is completed. The team meets to discuss its performance and identifies 'what went right' and 'what went wrong'. The audit ensures that the trip met the project's objectives and was completed within the agreed parameters of costs and time.

- Support. Ongoing support is provided to staff on how to engage with overseas students, taking into consideration cultural aspects and matching their backgrounds with suitable courses.

PROJECT RISK AND REWARDS

Risk monitoring and control is required throughout the project's life cycle. This determines the acceptability of the level of project risk in comparison with project expenditure and value. Initially, risks are high because they are not fully defined but, as the project progresses, they gradually reduce as more certainty about them is gained. Eventually, opportunities are realised for positive risks and threats are prevented from negative risks when the project is delivered and project risks have been successfully managed.

The expenditure/value of the project undergoes a similar change but in the opposite direction. The initial financial exposure is relatively small as the project is still in the planning stage. As the project develops, more and more expenditure is incurred and the potential value of the project potential increases. The highest financial exposure is around the crossover of risks and the financial exposure. At this moment the project is nearing completion and risks have been identified, analysed and responses implemented. The crossover is indicated in Figure 8.2.

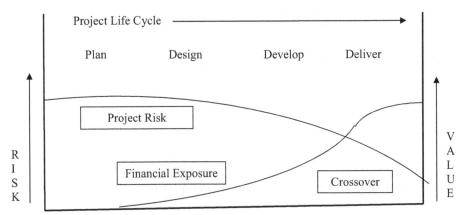

Figure 8.2   **Project risk and reward profile**

Importance of Project Risk Management

Project risk management plays a key role in achieving the project's objectives by identifying, analysing and responding to risks that impact on them throughout the life of a project. It plays a key role in selecting good projects, determining project scope and developing realistic estimates, thereby contributing to a successful project outcome. Through project risk identification and analysis, information is made available about the viability of the project and to support project planning. Project risk management identifies, and keeps stakeholders fully informed about, possible risk events and conditions. The major outcome of project risk management is an improved probability that project value realisation will be optimal and the project will be a success.

Unsatisfactory performance of project risk management can have negative outcomes. An unrealistic belief can be generated that all risks have been accounted for and that there are no further concerns. It may also cause the project to be shut down unnecessarily, thereby not realising the positive risks that may have been on offer. To avoid failure the organisation needs to be well aware that risk management is not free; it often adds substantial costs and time to the completion of the project.

A KNOWLEDGE AREA

Project risk management is regarded as the least mature of all project management knowledge areas (Schwalbe 2007). The reason is the high degree of interaction with all the other project knowledge areas. It is impossible to identify every possible project risk within these project areas because of the dynamic nature of projects. To demonstrate the diversity of possible project risk events, Figure 8.3 is provided. It gives examples of possible negative risk conditions that can be encountered in each of the project knowledge areas.

STRATEGIES FOR PROJECT RISK MANAGEMENT

According to PMBOK® (Project Management Institute 2008), project risk management can be defined as '[t]he systematic process of identifying, analyzing, and responding to project risk'. It is executed by completing the following steps: Risk Management Planning → Risk Identification → Qualitative/Quantitative Risk Analysis → Risk Response → Risk Monitoring and Control. In short, project risk management is the systematic process of identifying, analysing and responding to project risk.

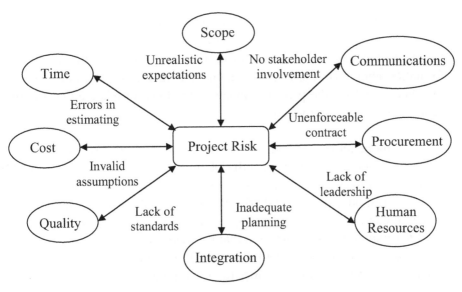

Figure 8.3   Project risk events/conditions across knowledge areas

Renn (2010) identified major requirements to complete each of the above processes in his 'transparent or inclusive' risk model. Planning is dependent on the capabilities of the project team and the standards it applies in structuring and developing the risk management plan. During the remaining risk management phases, social and economic factors come into play. The social aspects relate to the behaviour context in which the project is developed, while an economic approach seeks a rational and cost-effective outcome. For risk identification, a further factor needs consideration: politics. Risk identification is influenced by organisational power structures and agendas. Risk analysis requires additional technical expertise because of the quantitative nature of risk modelling.

Which factors and to what extent they play a role in risk management is determined by the perspective the organisation adopts. There are choices in how it shapes project risk management strategies. The 'governance' perspective suits project-oriented organisations since the aim is to maximise the probability and consequences of positive project risk events and minimise the effects of adverse risk events on project objectives. An 'asset' perspective could be applied in an engineering-type organisation. Because engineering practices are seen to be predictable it is possible to maximise the returns on its project investment. Bureaucratic organisations and government entities could favour the 'client' perspective to provide superior service to customers/public. Emphasis is placed on intangible benefits of project investments such as developing customer goodwill and social capital.

To be effective, project risk management should be 'practical' in its approaches. Obtaining adequate information is the key to success. Since the relationship between uncertainty and information is inverse, the better the information about risk the less uncertainty remains. It should, however, be remembered that for the project manager, conditions of relative uncertainty (partial information) are the rule.

Furthermore, the circumstances of a project can affect the risk management process, such as time pressure to get the job done and not being able to consult widely. By contrast, too many risk events may be identified and prevent satisfactory responses to the most critical risk events. While organisations will not deny the importance of risk management in today's volatile environment, the culture may not be supportive in that no serious attempt is being made to actually conduct a risk assessment. Because of perceived costs and the time it takes, there can be a natural resistance to formal project risk management.

KEY ISSUES IN PROJECT RISK MANAGEMENT

To determine where to put project management time and resources, the author (Fink 2012) surveyed members of the AIPM to establish key project risk issues, defined as those that require special attention over the next three to five years. This may be due to not understanding the nature of risk due to complexity, continued difficulty in managing the risk issue, and expected changes in project risk management. A detailed discussion of the study and its findings is provided in Appendix 1. The findings of the survey established the top ten project risk issues shown in Table 8.1.

Table 8.1   Ranking of project risk management issues

Rank	Issues
1	Understanding the risk concept
2	Agreeing on project risk
3	Recognising risk events
4	Developing a risk management approach
5	Preparing the risk management plan
6	Preparing the risk breakdown structure
7	Determining risk tolerance
8	Developing organisational risk processes
9	Estimating risk severity
10	Creating and updating the risk register

The table indicates the importance of understanding the project risk concept and related issues. They occupy ranks 1, 2, 3, and 7, and are covered in Chapter 7. The remaining key issues are the processes and outputs of project risk management, and are covered in this chapter.

The Project Risk Management Plan

The risk management plan describes the approach to be used on the project for risk management. It shows 'how' to identify risks, perform qualitative and/or quantitative analysis, develop risk responses, and monitor and control project risk activities. It is the plan for conducting project risk management. Planning should be a team approach so that consensus exists about the direction for the project.

PROJECT RISK PLANNING

It is an old saying that states: 'Plan for the Planning'. Risk planning should be appropriate for the project and common-sense questions are asked.

Example of Questions and Answers for Project Risk Planning

The kinds of questions and answers that reflect the earlier example of the university's overseas student recruitment project could be as follows:

- How risky is the project? For each recruitment drive, the university has to determine the level of risk. When severe demonstrations were experienced in a particular part of the world, the risk of visiting there would have increased because of the possibility of repeat demonstrations during the trip.

- Is it a new venture or something the organisation is familiar with? Travelling overseas would be familiar to university staff since they have attended fairs previously. However, destinations vary.

- Are there past projects to reference? The answer would be a qualified 'yes', depending on the similarities between the current and past recruitment projects.

- What is the visibility of the project? Overseas student recruitment is a highly visible project because the university is dependent on attracting overseas students. The university would want the project to be a success.

> • How big is the project? The project is of medium size since only a limited number of staff travel and the budget would be relatively small to cover costs of travel, accommodation and registration.
>
> • How important is the project? As stated above, such projects are important for the sustained success of the university.

INPUTS TO THE PROJECT RISK PLAN

To bring a systematic approach to developing the project risk plan, PMBOK® (Project Management Institute 2008) suggested that planning should identify the inputs to developing the plan. Types of inputs to risk management planning are as follows:

- Enterprise environmental factors. A SWOT analysis is an example of how to evaluate environmental factors. As previously discussed, this covers strengths (core capabilities, performance advantage, differentiators), weaknesses (uncertainty in required performance improvements), opportunities (positive project risk) and threats (competition, change, crisis, financial difficulties).

- Organisational processes. These are varied and include existing policies on risk tolerance and attitudes, agreed terms and concepts, people responsible for risk management, and standard templates and methodologies.

- Project scope statement. The statement describes the deliverables of the project and the work required in enough detail to provide a common understanding for stakeholders. Using the earlier example of a university sending staff overseas to recruit students, the project scope statement could include the following: the aim is to 'successfully recruit overseas students'; the deliverables are 'signed student course acceptances'; and success is defined as 'a high number of acceptances'.

- Project management plan. The plan describes how the project is to be executed, monitored, controlled and closed. It includes the processes, tools and techniques and outputs that are applicable to project risk management.

THE PROJECT RISK PLAN

For the plan itself, many questions should be answered. The following are some obvious ones and they are not exhaustive. What should the plan include? How will project risks be identified, quantified or qualified? What method(s) of risk modelling will be used? How is project risk linked to the work breakdown structure? How will risk responses be implemented? What are the monitoring processes for project risk management? Who is doing what and how often? Serious consideration needs to be given to determining when a risk is really a risk (see Chapter 7). From a management perspective the plan includes documenting and reporting requirements, and performance monitoring and tracking strategies.

Project Risk Modelling and Ranking

When confronted by risk, the inconsistency between different possible outcomes creates uncertainty about which outcome(s) will in fact materialise. To reduce uncertainty, risk analysis is conducted: project risks are identified, their potential impacts on the project's objectives and the probability of them occurring are estimated, and a range of potential responses is determined.

While uncertainty can be reduced as much as possible, it can never be eliminated; to accurately predict the future requires us to predict future opportunities and potential problems. Even our best attempts are not uniform as various perspectives will exist. Risk may be very clear to some but not to others and hence consensus is difficult to achieve. The process of risk analysis can be time consuming and its value and benefits are not always clear to senior management.

QUALITATIVE AND QUANTITATIVE ANALYSIS

Qualitative assessment differs from the quantitative approach in two fundamental ways. These are illustrated by reference to the earlier example of university staff travelling overseas for student recruitment. First, qualitative analysis is subjective. Assessing the risk of a staff member performing adequately overseas will produce different outcomes, in that one person may think highly of the person in question while another person may not think so highly. Second, the analysis uses an educated guess. The rating of the person's performance is based on perceptions such as past experiences with that person and likes and dislikes. At best, the outcome is a 'guesstimate' since there is not enough factual data available to make an accurate assessment.

To assist in developing a qualitative assessment of project risks, reference is made to the following documents:

- Organisational process assets. By assets is meant available data and documents. These can take many shapes and may include data about risk encountered in past projects and lessons learned from completed projects. Documentation in the form of standards and templates provide guidance for identifying project risk, assigning probabilities and determining risk severity.

- Project scope statement. This document is crucial in all project activities since it outlines the nature of the project, its activities and deliverables. For common or recurrent types of project, risk is generally well understood. For complex projects, such as those involving state-of-the-art technology, there is greater uncertainty and hence greater risk. This should be explicitly acknowledged in the project scope statement.

- Risk management plan. This is a key document for project risk management as outlined earlier in the chapter. The plan shows how project risk management will be conducted and refers to roles and responsibilities, the schedule of activities and possible risk categories.

- Risk register. A document that contains information about project risk events and conditions. It is usually displayed in a table or spreadsheet format and will be introduced in a later section.

The quantitative approach differs from the qualitative approach by its focus on numbers and use of numerical and/or statistical analysis. It is often preceded by qualitative risk analysis because this enables the project team to identify critical risks which are then subjected to the quantitative risk analysis approach. Quantitative risk analysis includes the following:

- Expert judgement. Experts have in-depth knowledge of the project and/or extensive experiences with similar projects and associated risk analysis. They are asked to participate in a Delphi study in which they evaluate potential risks via a questionnaire. Responses are collected, ranked and sent back for another round of evaluation.

After about three rounds, consensus is reached among the group on the project risks that exist and their severity.

- Sensitivity analysis. This approach measures the sensitivity of project objectives to changes in one project variable (i.e. risk) while holding all other variables constant. Sensitivity analysis determines which risks have the largest potential impact on project objectives. The approach is also called a 'what if?' analysis and uses spreadsheet software to carry out the analysis for various scenarios.

- Expected monetary value analysis. The expected monetary value is the product of two numbers: risk event probability (a number between 0 and 100) and risk event value (the amount of money to be gained or lost if the event occurs). The worked example in Table 8.2 shows how cost and probability can be used to calculate the expected value of the project. For each of three alternatives the costs are established and probabilities assigned. The total of probabilities equals 100. By multiplying cost and probability, the earned value of each option is calculated and compared to determine the most attractive option, in this case option B.

- Decision tree analysis. This approach is similar to 'earned monetary value analysis' in concept but differs in presentation. It uses a tree structure where each branch is a possible option. Various options are evaluated by considering their probabilities and impacts. Outcomes are compared and the most favourable is selected.

- Simulation. A project risk simulation uses a model that evaluates the impact of risk, specified at a detailed level, on objectives that are expressed at the project level. An example is Monte Carlo analysis, where a model's outcome is simulated many times to provide a statistical distribution of the calculated results.

Table 8.2   Expected monetary value analysis

Alternative	Cost	Probability	Earned Value
A - Optimistic	$100,000	0.20	$20,000
B - Most likely	$130,000	0.60	$78,000
C - Pessimistic	$180,000	0.20	$36,000
	Total	1.00	$134,000

COMPLEXITY OF RISK ANALYSIS

There are a number of strategies for completing risk analysis (Renn 2010). The traditional approach uses intuitive heuristic and judgement processes to determine risk probabilities and impacts. More specifically, 'rule of thumb' guidelines would have been developed and previous experiences would also be applied. In another strategy, importance is placed on contextual factors in forming perceptions about risk characteristics and the risk situation. In a further strategy, the use of semantics determines risk sources, people and the circumstances of the situation. The way risk is described and communicated plays a critical role in risk analysis. A complicating factor is the trust and credibility of the actors involved in the risk debate. The chosen strategy should align closely with approaches commonly used within the organisation in order to gain acceptance.

Complexity is further increased by psychological factors that influence the estimation of risk probabilities (Renn 2010):

- Availability bias. Probability is likely to be overestimated if the individual recognises risk easily and quickly or is aware of the risk. The example given is that if news is readily available about people being killed by lightning strikes, then the risk of being struck by lightning is regarded as particularly significant.

- Anchoring effect. Probability will also be overestimated if a risk is associated with known events. For example, if waste is known to be incinerated an association is formed between waste and its toxic nature and harmfulness to the environment. This is despite the lack of knowledge about the incineration process and/or the nature of the waste being disposed of.

- Distribution of risk over time. Risk probability is underestimated if risk events are spread over time rather than all occurring at once. This can be illustrated by the occurrence of road accidents throughout the year rather than all happening at once. The public appears to accept the existence of road accidents and attributes a lower probability of occurrence than if they thought accidents were concentrated in a short period of time.

- Assessment bias. It was found that uncertainty about losses resulting from risk events causes the assessment of loss to be close to the median of losses (i.e. the size of loss that occurs most often). As a result, low risks are overestimated and high risks are underestimated.

Complexity, however, can be moderated by introducing a degree of pragmatism into risk analysis. Renn (2010: 3) made the following suggestions. First, avoid 'making all risk judgements subjective reflections of power and interest'. These are examples of biases that distort the outcomes of risk analysis. They can be conscious or unconscious and it is the task of the project risk manager to find out if bias is a significant issue. Hopkinson (2011) makes the point that bias is often caused by organisational pressures to support a preferred profile of the project viz. its costs and objectives. Most pressure appears to be at the pre-approval stage when the project sponsor and team are anxious to proceed with the project.

Second, confirm that the 'task of risk managers is to provide evidence-based information' in support of risk analysis. At project approval it is tempting to make optimistic and even pessimistic adjustments to the information that is presented (Hopkinson 2011). With the former, the positive aspects of the project are over-emphasised, such as relying on 'best-case' rather than realistic scenarios of project outcomes. As a consequence, the project may be difficult to develop within the promised specifications. A pessimistic bias can exist when the project environment is such that serious consequences result when projects do not meet their stated objectives.

Third, accept that while risk assessments are based on observations and perceptions or social constructions of the world, they will have to be justified by logical reasoning (Renn 2010). For example, an economic (financial) approach can be followed during the construction of the project business case as outlined in Chapter 4. A business case takes into account risks that could impact on estimated project costs and benefits and calculates a net figure to indicate a potential positive return on the investment (benefits exceed costs) or a negative return, which could cause the project to be rejected. Senior management is generally familiar with and supportive of this line of reasoning.

RANKING OF PROJECT RISK SEVERITY

The relationship between probability and impact determines risk severity.

> **Example of Determining Project Risk Severity**
>
> To illustrate the approach, reference is again made to the earlier example of a university sending its staff overseas to recruit students. The team believes that costs will increase due to higher oil prices, and that air fares may go up by 10%. They estimate the impact on their travel plan to be in the medium range, a 2 on a scale of 5, because fewer staff may be allowed to travel. The team also determines the probability of the increase to be 1 on a 5-point scale, which is low because there has been a drop in the number of people travelling by air recently and airlines would be reluctant to increase their fares. According to the intersection of probability and impact (probability = 1, impact = 2) in Figure 8.4, the risk severity is at a moderate threshold.

Risk Severity Classification Assessment

Risk Severity Assessment Matrix

H = High severity. There will be a major disruption and a different project approach is required.

M = Moderate severity. Some disruption will be experienced which may require a different project approach.

L = Low severity. There is minimum impact and management attention is required to ensure project risk remains low.

Probability \ Impact	1	2	3	4	5
1	M	M	H	H	H
2	L	M	M	H	H
3	L	M	M	H	H
4	L	L	L	M	M
5	L	L	L	L	L

Figure 8.4   Risk severity assessment

Risk severity is more graphically expressed in colour. The above example would indicate a moderate (yellow) value. The other colours are green (low) and red (high). Colours are traditionally associated with our feelings of danger and send a powerful signal to management on the severity of the risk.

The probability–impact grid provides a single risk rating for each risk event or condition. This proves a convenient indication for the risk manager as to where to focus his/her attention: the high-rated versus the low-rated risks. However, Ward (1999) provided warnings for this approach. The risk rating calculated by the impact score times the probability score has no absolute meaning. A numeric value is appealing and gives the impression of objectivity, but it cannot be interpreted that one risk is exactly that much more important than another one. Adding up the numbers also does not give an indication of the overall amount of project risk. Within the grid, the ranges of ratings can overlap depending on the ranges chosen to indicate the severity of risk. This poses a conceptual problem and requires a decision on how thresholds should be classified as low, medium or high.

Ward (1999) suggested that a variety of impact factors could be applied to provide greater understanding of risk severity. This could lead to separate probability–impact grids for project costs, time and quality, for example. Management would thereby obtain a multi-dimensional assessment of risk, especially in the early stages of the project when the first indications about the nature of the possible risks are sought via their potential impact on various project activities.

Project Risk Register

The output of the risk identification process is a list of identified risk events/ conditions and other information needed to provide the context in which the risks can be managed. They are recorded in the project risk register and progressively refined during project risk management processes. The register is often displayed in a table or spreadsheet format.

RISK REGISTER CONTENTS

Risk events occur to the detriment or enhancement of the project and therefore need to be fully described. Common headings in the register are as follows:

- An identification number for each risk.

- A rank for each risk event/condition to indicate its level of severity.

- The name of each risk.

- A description of each risk event/condition.

- The category under which each risk falls.

- The root cause of each risk – the real or underlying reason why a problem/opportunity occurs.

- Triggers for each risk or indicators of risk.

- Potential responses to each risk.

- The risk owner or person who will take responsibility for each risk.

- The probability and impact of each risk occurring.

- The status of each risk, ranging from newly identified to having been resolved.

Example of a Project Risk Register

Earlier, the example was provided in which the risk of an increase in the cost of airfares was determined as moderate. Using this information and hypothetically allocating the risk an identification number and ranking, the entry in the project risk register could be as shown in Table 8.3.

Table 8.3   Sample entry in the project risk register

Content	Details
Identification number	12
Rank	26
Name	Airfares
Description	An increase in the cost of airfares
Category	Travelling
Root cause	International oil prices are on the increase
Trigger	Airline increases the cost of its tickets
Response strategy	Mitigate the risk by reducing the number of staff travelling
Owner	Student Recruitment Office
Probability	1 on a scale of 5
Impact	2 on a scale of 5
Status	No notification of cost increase has as yet been received

The structure of the risk register has shortcomings (Ward 1999). If individual risk descriptions are not adequate it will create ambiguity and misunderstanding in the minds of the project team. Interdependencies between risks are not clearly indicated and the tabular form does not provide detail on the interaction between response strategies. Its tabular form and simplicity, however, assist management in gaining an overall feel for project risks.

Implementation of Project Risk Responses

The central theme of this book is to respond to the existence of project risks in a way that adds value. Chapter 2 identified different risk response strategies to protect the value of the organisation and/or create value. While the selection of appropriate responses is important, this is not in itself sufficient without giving attention to implementing these strategies during project risk management. The completion of both processes is critical to project success.

Risk responses decisions are usually made at a high level because of their significance to the project portfolio, while their implementation is at the lower project level. Being outside the decision-maker's direct control has created the concern within management that response strategies are actually implemented. Hopkinson (2011: 165) quoted the experiences of a corporate risk manager: 'In the past, my company has been very good at risk identification, risk assessment and risk filing.' Monitoring and control activities should ensure that project risk responses are actioned.

MONITORING INFORMATION

The main document for monitoring performance in implementing project risk responses is the risk management plan. It provides processes that should be followed as well as documentation and reporting requirements. The second important reference is the project risk register since it shows the progress that has been made for each of the identified risk events/conditions. Not only does it define project risk characteristics but also reports their current implementation status (see Table 8.3).

Performance reports communicate to management how project risk responses are developing according to the risk management plan. The reports compare actual achievements to the risk management plan in respect of project risk activities and deliverables at predefined project milestones. Reporting is the responsibility of the project manager (or nominee) and highlights compliance or deviation from the plan. Deviations can be caused by a change to the project itself, project activities uncovering new or changed risk events/conditions, or inadequately defined risk responses.

Variance and trend analysis provide deeper insights by assessing performance in different areas of project activities. For example, project costing should collect and report on the cost of implementing risk responses. Variations, both good and bad, from the original estimation will have to be carefully considered. When the variation is significant it raises a difficult question: should the risk management plan be adjusted to include additional risk activities? This will affect the project's costs and possibly its viability. Alternatively, the temptation may arise to ignore the new situation and avoid making changes in project risk responses.

To lessen the impact of changes, a project risk reserve could be established. Reserves are funds set aside by management for future risk events, and generally refer to the 'known unknowns' of risk. As outlined in Chapter 7, project risk is easier to identify, manage and monitor where information is complete ('known knowns') than when uncertainty is high (the 'known unknowns') or extreme ('unknown unknowns'). It is not possible to predict these risks in detail except to provide a 'reserve' to cater for risk exposure that may occur in future. Reserve analysis compares the remaining reserves (cost and schedule) with the impact of new risk responses. Professional judgement is needed to assess the adequacy of the reserve at any one time because it is dependent on the amount of yet undiscovered risks in the project.

CONTROL ACTIVITIES

Projects are not static and are periodically evaluated for new risks. Any new risk should be assessed and a change request submitted for approval. The requested change needs to be analysed, its consequences documented and approved, and recorded in the risk register, risk response plan and risk management plan. The risk response is funded from the risk response reserve or, if this is absent or inadequate, through a 'workaround'. This attempts to overcome risks that have emerged by thinking of a response as an alternative to previously determined responses.

Example of Project Risk Response Implementation

In the earlier example of university staff travelling overseas to recruit students there is the risk of missing the flight because of potential traffic jams. The project team has two risk response strategies to choose from. First, if it is critical not to miss the flight, it should avoid the risk of traffic jams. It can check on traffic conditions just prior to departure and choose a route free from traffic congestion. If it wants to reduce the risk, it could arrive at the airport area the night before but may still be caught in a traffic jam when travelling to the airport. The risk is not voided but mitigated. Should the team be confronted by an unexpected traffic jam for which they had not planned a response, the contingency plan would be activated. In it, alternate ways of getting to the airport would have been identified. For example, if there is a high urgency to get to the airport, a helicopter service could be used. To cover costs, funds in the reserve are used. Alternatively, the team has to 'work around' the problem by selecting an alternate route to the airport by trial and error. This is, however, a risky response strategy.

The Project Team

A diverse range of factors influence the social processes operating within project teams. Cicmil et al. (2006: 676) referred to this as project actuality: 'the understanding of the lived experience of organisational members with work and life in their local project environment'. How the team acts and behaves is continuously influenced by how they perceive and experience contextual influences. These could include observed power relations, the quality of interpersonal communications and collaboration, the style of managerial control and the degree of tensions created by project diversity.

FUNCTIONING OF TEAM

While professional guidelines are comprehensive in prescribing processes to be followed, it is not clear what impact they have on the functioning of the project team. Through an extensive literature review, Sewchurran et al. (2010: 682) found a 'lack of correlation between prescribed practice and as-lived experiences'. It appears that performance is determined by the team's current and past experiences with project situations (Cicmil et al. 2006). This includes avoiding elements of dysfunction caused by the following factors (Barkley 2004):

- Absence of trust. Team members should be able to work with each other without the fear of being deceived and undermined. Trust has many meanings including reliability, integrity, competence, all of which are personal traits that are highly desirable in project activities.

- Fear of conflict. Disagreement in an aggressive form takes attention away from the project because time and energy are devoted to resolving conflict. It not only involves team members but also the valuable time of management.

- Lack of commitment. There is a difference between 'participating in' and 'committing to' the project. The latter implies accepting responsibility for completing project tasks. Commitment at the project management level is particularly important as it indicates that the project manager stands behind the project and will accept both the recognition, as well as possible blame, for the outcome of the project.

- Avoidance of accountability. As part of their commitment, project members should be expected to analyse their actions, be prepared to admit to making mistakes, seek to develop solutions to problems, and work within time and budget constraints. When reporting on progress there should be honesty in their feedback.

- Inattention to tasks. Projects are driven by work breakdown structures which break down the activities of the project into individual tasks. Meticulously carrying out tasks will provide a solid foundation for project development and, when aggregated, ensure project completion on time.

SOCIAL FACTORS AND MOTIVATION

Project members carry out multiple roles, often work on different projects at the same time, and experience the inherent uncertainty of tenure. On the other hand, the dynamic nature of projects provides opportunities for gaining new knowledge, skills and experiences. To manage this diversity, project managers are giving increasing attention to the psychology of project work, including its social aspects and motivations.

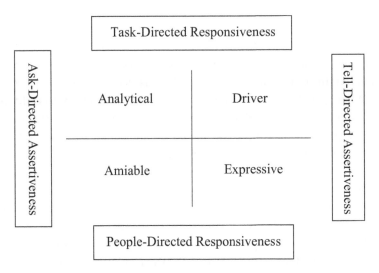

Figure 8.5   Social styles profile

Social factors provide the harmony in which team members are able to work effectively with each other on project activities. This is largely determined by personalities for which a number of models exist (see Schwalbe 2007):

- According to the Social Styles Profile (see Figure 8.5), people fall primarily into one of four zones, based on their assertiveness and responsiveness. Those on opposite corners (Drivers and Amiables, Analyticals and Expressives) may have difficulties getting along.

- Under the 'DISC' profile, behaviour is reflected in a four-dimensional model of Dominance, Influence, Steadiness and Compliance. People in opposite quadrants can have problems understanding each other.

- The Meyers–Briggs Type Indicator (MBTI) is a popular tool for determining personality preferences and helping teammates understand each other. The four dimensions include Extrovert/ Introvert (E/I), Sensation/Intuition (S/N), Thinking/Feeling (T/F) and Judgement/Perception (J/P).

Understanding social factors is useful for matching the requirements of project risk management with a suitable personality. Using the Social Styles profile it could be argued that an 'expressive' approach is best suited during project risk planning. Planning and the plan itself have to be conducted and completed with a high degree of visibility. During risk identification, the 'ask-directed' strategy of an 'amiable' personality is appropriate because risk events/conditions have to be discovered through enquiries. Risk analysis is clearly suited to an 'analytical' person. When developing risk responses, the 'driver' approach could be used because the project team receives direction to apply the selected risk responses. Finally, risk monitoring is best conducted by an 'amiable' personality since it seeks to discover, by asking, areas that require attention.

In addition to recognising the impact of social factors, motivation plays an important role in completing project work. There are many theories on motivation, including Maslow's Hierarchy of Needs, McClelland's Acquired-Needs theory, and McGregor's Theory X and Y. A common distinction is between intrinsic ('I play the piano because I enjoy it') and extrinsic ('my parents required me to play the piano') motivation. Intrinsic motivation causes people to participate in an activity for their own enjoyment while extrinsic motivation causes people to do something for a reward or to avoid a penalty.

In Herzberg's Motivational and Hygiene Factors theory, motivational factors produce job satisfaction through actual achievement, recognition of the work done, the nature of work itself, the degree of responsibility given to do the work, and prospects for advancement and personal growth. Hygiene factors themselves will cause dissatisfaction if not present, but do not motivate workers to do more. Examples include larger salaries, more supervision and an attractive work environment.

Both factors should be satisfied, but motivational factors are significant because of the type of person attracted to project risk management. They value the diversity of work and the challenges it provides. Issues are numerous and interrelated and involve a high degree of subjectiveness in their evaluation. The concept of project risk is difficult to grasp and determined by perceptions and judgements. Each project produces a unique product or service with its own set of risk events and conditions.

Conclusion

This chapter identified, described and provided examples of what are regarded essential project risk management processes, inputs and outputs. It demonstrated how import project risk management is to all of the knowledge areas of project management. Since project risk management is regarded as less 'mature' in its practice, a comprehensive project risk management plan is required. This will guide approaches to risk modelling and ranking, as well as developing project risk responses. It is critical that risk responses are actually implemented during project development. The chapter perceived the project register as a core document because it acts as a repository for information about project risk events and conditions and the progress towards implementing responses. Finally, it is argued that without a motivated project team, project risk management may not succeed.

9

Project Risk Governance Maturity

Introduction

Organisations can use a framework or model to guide them in achieving effective and efficient PRG. They are able not only to determine their current strengths and weaknesses but also to identify the scope for improvements. The model itself contains dimensions against which maturity is measured at each stage of development, from an early to a mature stage. It is commonly referred to as a maturity model since it provides a roadmap for achieving governance sophistication.

Project Management Maturity Models

The emergence of maturity models can be attributed to the increasing number of project managers in the 1990s, when organisations recognised that they would best be managed in project mode (Outperform 2012). Just relying on the performance of project managers, however, did not assure the long-term and consistent performance of project activities. It was recognised that in addition to project management activities at the individual project level, attention to projects at the corporate level was required. Hence, a number of models emerged indicating that project management had achieved a new level of maturity.

SCOPE AND EXAMPLES OF MODELS

Outperform (2012) defined a maturity model as follows: 'A maturity model is a structured collection of elements that describe characteristics of effective processes.' A more holistic definition was offered by Schlichter et al. (2010): 'Maturity models are standards that shape institutional designs and management practices as well as social norms and expectations about behaviour [and] defines excellence in a particular domain and steps to achieve it.' In essence, a maturity model provides a starting point for determining organisational maturity. Its design and content is based on a community's prior experiences with what constitutes maturity. It uses a common language and aims to provide a shared vision for improvements that are necessary and the prioritisation of actions.

The Capability Maturity Model (CMM) is often regarded as the foundation on which subsequent maturity models are based. Yeo and Ren (2009: 276) recognised its broad scope: CMM 'has been applied to many aspects of organizational, human resource, people, and product development as a means of assessment and as part of a framework for continuous improvement.' Among project management professionals, two models are popular: the UK Government's Portfolio, Programme and Project Management Maturity Model (P3M3®) and PMI's Organisational Project Management Maturity Model (OPM3®). They are briefly outlined below.

Portfolio, Programme and Project Management Maturity Model (P3M3®)

The Portfolio, Programme and Project Management Maturity Model is offered by the Office of Government Commerce, a department within the UK Government. It was described by Outperform (2012) as

> a reference guide for structured best practice. It breaks down the broad disciplines of portfolio, programme and project management into a hierarchy of Key Process Areas (KPAs). The hierarchical approach enables organisations to assess their current capability and then plot a roadmap for improvement prioritised by those KPAs which will make the biggest impact on performance.

The hierarchical structure of KPAs is important since it enables the organisation to move from a low, immature level to a high, mature level. Thirty-two KPAs are distributed across five levels defined from 'initial' to 'optimised'. In the first level, some recognition is given to the role of projects within the organisation. At the 'repeatable' stage, each project is managed to a specified minimum standard. When the organisation has its own centralised controlled project processes it has reached the 'defined' level. Projects become 'managed' when specific measurements for project performance are applied. Finally, during the 'optimised' level, continuous process improvement with proactive problem and technology management takes place.

The 32 KPAs cover functional achievement/process goals, approach, deployment, review, perception and performance measures. Outperform (2012) provide examples of KPAs found in a business case, which is part of the 'repeatable' stage:

- Goal. Establish a framework to support planning and management of a change and benefits realisation.

- Approach. Appoint a senior person to be responsible for the business case.

- Deployment. Complete a business justification and align the case with strategic objectives.

- Review. Monitor and review the progress at the project programme and project levels.

- Perception. Seek views of stakeholders about the desirability and achievability of the project.

- Performance measures. Obtain ongoing information about the project's value for money and achievability.

Improvements are brought about by breaking down the project goals into manageable tasks. Four generic steps are involved (Outperform 2012): 'where are you today?' (the baseline assessment); 'where do you want to be?' (applying KPAs); 'how will you get there?' (the improvement roadmap); and 'how will you know?' (the maturity assessment).

Organisational Project Management Maturity Model (OPM3®)

As a measure of effective project governance, PMI developed OPM3®. Its purpose is described at Wikipedia (2013) as providing 'a method for organizations to understand their Organizational Project Management processes and measure their capabilities in preparation for improvement'. It integrates the three domains of organisational project management, namely portfolio, programme and project management, into one maturity model. Maturity is equated to improvements across a wide range of activities including developing business strategy, estimating project costs and benefits, and managing technology.

Schlichter et al. (2010) identified the strength of OPM3® as identifying specific capabilities which make up best practices and the dependencies between them. For this reason they refer to OPM3® as a CMM: capability statements are regarded as essential because without them the model does not work. Each capability statement is 'elaborated by an outcome statement [and] each outcome statement is assigned a KPI'. Dependencies between capabilities result in a capability network with identified subsets grouped as 'best practices'. Schlichter et al. (2010) maintain that 'the term "best practice" was chosen for marketing purposes but denotes nothing but a container of capability statements'.

Unlike the hierarchical approach of P3M3®, OPM3® is implemented in a life cycle of assessment, improvement, and re-assessment.

OPM3® offers guidelines rather than prescriptions by focusing on three elements (Wikipedia 2013): knowledge, assessment and improvement. Knowledge is required to plan for the large numbers of best practices for organisational project management. Assessment guides the evaluation of current capabilities and identifies areas in need of improvement, while improvement lays out the steps to be followed to achieve performance improvement goals.

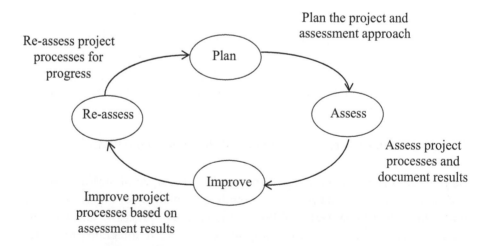

Figure 9.1   OPM3® life cycle

The challenge for the organisation is to adapt the models to support PRG principles. Because they are broadly designed it allows practices to be developed relevant to the needs of PRG.

Benefits of Maturity Assessment

Maturity models provide a roadmap ('the maturity path') of the stages to growth across specified dimensions, for achieving excellence in project management and governance. Progress along the path is assessed in an objective and methodical way, providing management with confidence in how the state of maturity was determined. Rad and Levin (2006: 2) referred to the approach as providing 'proactive internal pressures ... aimed at future improvements in performance, which in turn will result in improved profits'. In this way, maturity models become a framework for continuous organisational improvement and success.

The guidelines and best practices associated with maturity models support change management. They help to implement improvement plans in a transparent manner since they are based on dimensions and scales that have been agreed to within the organisation. Encouragement is provided for discussions among project stakeholders as to how best to progress along the maturity path. Communications and collaboration between them are thereby improved and they are satisfied that the organisation intends to move to a higher level of performance.

When pursuing the strategy of ongoing assessment of the organisation's maturity, the project management mode changes from reactive (reacting to a crisis in a project) to proactive (seeking continuous performance improvement). This is akin to transiting from the fire-fighting mode to a fire prevention mode (Rad and Levin 2006). The change requires measures of expected project performance, based on criteria for which quantitative data can be collected, to indicate whether or not project success has been achieved. A benchmark for the level of sophistication of current practices should be established against which future improvements can be determined.

Benefits of maturity assessment can be observed in the external environment (Rad and Levin 2006). It may satisfy a client, for whom the project is to be carried out, that the provider has achieved a desired level of maturity in order to be awarded the project. Alternatively, the bidding organisation may be able to demonstrate having achieved a maturity level beyond the one prescribed by the client, thereby providing a competitive advantage in the tendering process. This provides an excellent enterprise credential when confronted by competitors. It is important, however, that agreement exists between the provider and the client as to the validity and credibility of the maturity model being used.

While it is tempting for senior management to aim at achieving the highest level of maturity, Vandersluis (2004) warned that it may not always be the case that a higher level is better. He referred to the example whereby the cost of changing the internal culture through providing staff education and training may outweigh the potential benefits of improving the working climate within the organisation. Every organisation should find the level of maturity best suited to its current circumstances.

Checklist: Familiarity of the Organisation with Project Maturity Models

- Is the organisation familiar with current project management maturity models?

- Does the organisation use a project management maturity model?

- To what extent has the model been adapted to the organisation's project characteristics?

- Are the advantages of using a project management maturity model understood?

- Is project management maturity regularly assessed?

- Does the project management maturity model provide a useful roadmap for improvement?

- Is the transition to a higher level of project management maturity carefully considered?

Maturity Levels and Dimensions

Maturity models are designed as a matrix. The horizontal axis represents levels of maturity, also referred to as stages of growth. They are assessed against dimensions which are represented on the vertical axis. Dimensions are categories of criteria against which the maturity level is measured. Criteria are defined for each of the maturity levels.

LEVELS

Maturity levels are numbered on a scale where the lowest number indicates the lowest maturity. The levels themselves are broadly described and vary across disciplines. The IT Governance Maturity Model (ITGI 2003) is a good example of how levels can be described when expressed in generic terms.

Governance performance is rated on a scale to grade its maturity level, from nonexistent (zero) to optimised (five). The non-existent stage indicates there are no governance processes since the topic has not yet been addressed. During the initial stage, some evidence of an ad hoc approach to governance is apparent. The organisation recognises the need for governance but processes are sporadic and applied on a case-by-case basis. There appears to be no governance structure in place. When governance processes become more consistent in stage three, they are repeatedly performed and follow a recognisable pattern. However, the effectiveness of governance structures depends on the performance of key individuals and their particular expertise.

Governance reaches the next stage when processes are standardised and documented but are mainly based on existing procedures. They are expected to be followed although little monitoring takes place. The governance structure is improved in that training takes place and communication is encouraged. In stage four, management monitors the performance of governance and takes corrective actions where and when necessary. There is a positive attitude to continuous improvement and processes are automated as much as possible. Finally, the optimised stage indicates a high level of good practice and governance performance compares well with those in similar organisations.

Table 9.1   Levels in a generic maturity model

Stage	Description
0 Non-existent	Complete lack of any recognisable processes. The enterprise has not even recognised that there is an issue to be addressed.
1 Initial/ad hoc	There is evidence that the enterprise has recognised that the issues exist and need to be addressed. There are, however, no standardised processes; instead, there are ad hoc approaches that tend to be applied on an individual or case-by-case basis. The overall approach to management is disorganised.
2 Repeatable but intuitive	Processes have developed to the stage where similar procedures are followed by different people undertaking the same task. There is no formal training or communication of standard procedures, and responsibility is left to the individual. There is a high degree of reliance on the knowledge of individuals and, therefore, errors are likely.
3 Defined processes	Procedures have been standardised and documented, and communicated through training. It is mandated that these processes should be followed; however, it is unlikely that deviations will be detected. The procedures themselves are not sophisticated but are the formalisation of existing practices.
4 Managed and measurable	Management monitors and measures compliance with procedures and take action where processes appear not to be working effectively. Processes are under constant improvement and provide good practice. Automation and tools are used in a limited or fragmented way.
5 Optimised	Processes have been refined to a level of good practice, based on the results of continuous improvement and maturity modelling in comparison with other enterprises. Approaches are integrated and automated as far as possible, enabling the organisation to adapt to changed circumstances.

There are a number of interpretations of what constitutes the levels in a Project Management Maturity (PMM) model. For example, Kwak and Ibbs (2002) determined each maturity level by major project management processes, organisational characteristics and key focus areas:

- Level 1: Ad hoc. There are no project management processes and project management lacks senior management support. The aim is to initiate basic project management processes.

- Level 2: Planned. At this stage, project management processes are informally defined and a weak team-oriented approach is applied. Projects are individually planned.

- Level 3: Managed at project level. Formal project planning and control is practised but still at the individual project level. Project teams are starting to emerge but training is informal.

- Level 4: Managed at corporate level. The focus is on project programme management with a strong teamwork approach and supported by formal project management training. Planning and control incorporates multiple projects.

- Level 5: Continuous learning. The organisation seeks to continuously improve and innovate its project management processes since it has become project-driven and responsive to market demands.

Vandersluis (2004) proposed a five-level model designed for general purpose projects. Its stages are summarised as follows:

- Level 1: Ad hoc. Project management is carried out on a project-by-project basis in a non-standard manner. According to the authors, most organisations appeared to fall into this category when the research was conducted.

- Level 2: Planned. Some planning standards for projects exist but projects are tracked on a project-by-project basis.

- Level 3: Managed. There is some evidence of a standardised approach to both project planning and tracking.

- Level 4: Integrated. Project management is brought together for all projects.

- Level 5: Sustained. There exists a re-iterative process to self-correct and self-improve project management so that it is self-sustaining.

A number of observations can be made from the above project management maturity models. The level descriptions are similar, with the first level recognising an 'ad hoc' approach and the final level an 'optimised' state. At the beginning there are no formal processes, while in the final stage processes are firmly established and continuously improved. Project and business activities are aligned in organisation-wide practices. In between is the 'initial' level in which there is some indication of project management planning and presence of processes. During the following 'managed' level, a formal approach to project management exists and is applied to every project. Prior to reaching the optimised level stage, project management is formalised and integrated, and takes on corporate characteristics with the focus on project programme management and the move towards a PBO.

For complex projects, including risk management capabilities, Yeo and Ren (2009) proposed a five-level maturity model. The 'Risk Management Capability Maturity Model (RM-CMM) for Complex Product Systems' recognised the following levels:

- Level 1: Ad hoc. There is no structured approach to deal with risk as there is a lack of awareness about risk management. Management mindsets are reactive and mechanistic and come into play after the problem has occurred. There are no procedures to deal with the unexpected.

- Level 2: Initial. Some awareness exists about the importance of risk management and its potential benefits. Project risk management processes and structures are of a rudimentary nature.

- Level 3: Defined. This is the watershed stage (referred to as the 'demarcation level') in which formal risk management is included in corporate business processes. Generic risk management produces policies and procedures that are implemented organisation-wide. The system deals with most known or predictable risks, but senior management are beginning to understand the benefits of project risk management. The organisation emphasises project management within a balanced matrix structure.

- Level 4: Managed. Risk management processes are clearly defined to identify, assess and respond to risks. Risk impact and severity are measured and risk management performance is monitored. There is a risk-aware mindset with a proactive approach to the management of risks, and consideration is given to both internal and external stakeholders. There is likely to be a strong PBO.

- Level 5: Optimising. The alignment between project and business objectives ensures that business risks are seriously considered. There is a comprehensive risk management plan with qualitative and quantitative measures for risk assessment. Testing innovative ideas and exploring the potential of new approaches to conducting business and associated risks are encouraged. The organisation structure is clearly project-based and therefore highly flexible and responsive to market changes.

Table 9.2   Dimensions of project risk governance

Constructs of PRG Maturity	Variables of PRG Maturity
Projects in Organisations	Project- versus Product-Based Organisation The Project-Based Organisation (PBO): Implications, Advantages, Complexities PBO Structures
Business and Project Interaction	Business Strategy Formulation Business and Project Strategy Alignment Strategies for Value-Protecting Strategies for Value-Creating Alignment with Project Risk Management
Corporate and Project Governance	The Concept of Governance Corporate Governance Conformance and Performance Project Governance
Project Risk Governance – Processes	Scope of Project Risk Governance Portfolio, Programme and Project Management Investment Management Value Realisation Performance Management
Project Risk Governance – Structures and Relationships	Organisational Leadership and Board of Directors Project Sponsors and Project Managers Steering Committees and Project Management Office Linking Structures and Processes
Project Risk Governance in Context	Professional Associations Risk Management Standards Project Success Human Resources Management Change Management Paradigmatic Influences
The Concept of Project Risk	What is Project Risk? – The Basics Project Risk – A Deeper Perspective Perceptions of Project Risk Project Risk and Uncertainty Project Risk Appetite and Tolerance
Essentials of Project Risk Management	Understanding Projects Importance of Project Risk Management Project Risk Management Plan Project Risk Modelling and Ranking Project Risk Register Implementing Project Risk Responses Project Team
Project Risk Governance Maturity	Project Management Maturity Models Benefits of Maturity Assessment Maturity Levels and Dimensions A PRG Maturity Model Progressing between PRG Maturity Levels

DIMENSIONS

Which level of maturity has been reached is determined by comparing project management/governance processes, structures and relationships against consistent and easy-to-understand dimensions. The use of dimensions greatly simplifies the task of initiating improvements since they provide a pragmatic and structured approach for measuring how well developed is an enterprise's project management or governance. They reflect a capability benchmark against which the organisation can rate itself to establish its strengths and weaknesses.

Project risk governance dimensions can be developed by first identifying constructs and then variables within them. For PRG, the chapter headings of this book provide suitable constructs, while the topics within each chapter represent variables. An overview of PRG dimensions developed by this approach is presented in Table 9.2.

A Project Risk Governance Maturity Model

Chapter 2 introduced the cyclical approach to aligning business and project strategies and activities. Four stages were identified: formulating strategic goals ('what should be done'), deciding on the project portfolio, programmes and projects ('what can be done'), implementing PRG ('how to do it') and managing risks at the project level ('do it'). The cycle is completed by adding a reflection stage on 'what was done' during the implementation of PRG. This stage supports an assessment of PRG maturity and is included in the augmented PRG model as shown in Figure 9.2.

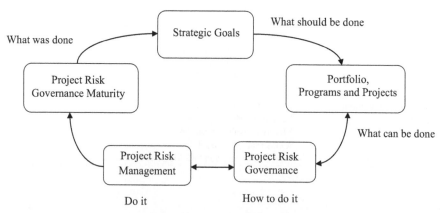

Figure 9.2   Augmented project risk governance model

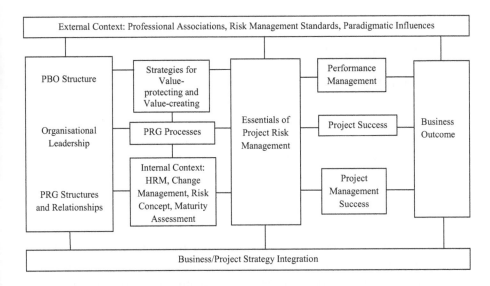

Figure 9.3   Relationships between project risk governance maturity dimensions

Levels of PRG maturity are determined according to governance performance in the dimensions identified in Table 9.2. To understand the relative impact of each dimension on PRG maturity, they are represented in a model as shown in Figure 9.3. At one end of the model are the organisational factors that determine the approaches to PRG. They are the characteristics of a PBO, organisational leadership to implement governance and supporting PRG structures and relationships. At the opposite end are the contributions that PRG makes in the form of business outcomes.

In between are the activities of PRG processes to implement project risk strategies for value-creating and value-protecting. Project development itself requires effective project risk management. Both PRG processes and project risk management are moderated by the internal context such as HRM practices and the ability to manage change. Performance is assessed through performance criteria and success factors. There are two ongoing influences: the external context and business/project integration. The former is largely outside the organisation's control but needs to be considered during PRG. The latter provides the overriding objective of PRG, namely to achieve improved business outcomes by linking projects with business strategy.

There are five levels, each with variations in PRG performance within each of the dimensions. The details are provided in Appendix 3. Below are the key dimensions that make up each level.

LEVEL 1: AD HOC

At this early stage there is no or little awareness of PRG among executive management and it has not received recognition within the organisation. This may be due to a hands-off attitude of the board to risk matters and that no or few formal standards exist for ERM. The emphasis is on identifying and managing negative project risks, while the opportunities of positive project risks are not actively exploited.

The organisation operates in a traditional hierarchical and functional manner. When developing business strategy, little consideration is given to the role of projects. There is no or little recognition of project governance within the organisation's governance framework. Project management is guided by the hard paradigm and manages project costs and benefits and the most obvious associated negative risks. The implementation of project risk responses is neglected. While the concept of uncertainty in project outcomes is understood, project risk appetite and tolerance are inadequately defined. No or little use is made of project management maturity models.

LEVEL 2: INITIAL

During this stage the importance of project governance and PRG is starting to be recognised within the organisation. There is increasing project activity, and business strategy takes into account the importance of projects to business success. The board's attitude changes to one that attempts to balance control with innovation in relation to risk. The board and senior management realise the strategic importance of managing project risk. Existing risk management standards, such as ISO 31000, provide a guide for ERM. Emphasis is placed on diversifying the overall risk in the project portfolio.

At the project level, obvious opportunities present in positive project risks are now pursued. A more sophisticated approach is taken when considering the impact of project risk in project investments. The organisation gives attention to defining its project risk appetite and tolerance levels. Management, however, has concerns about the effectiveness of risk response implementation. It is understood that risk is not a phenomenon but is socially constructed. The importance of project risk management as a project management knowledge area is recognised and project members are encouraged to join project management associations. There is an emerging awareness of the soft project management paradigm and the merits of project management maturity models.

LEVEL 3: DEFINED

The move to a project-based environment sees the formulation of both business and project strategies with project risk management included in project strategy. At the board level, attention is given to PRG. Existing ERM systems contribute to defining PRG processes and structures. Value-protecting strategies are developed for preventable and external project risks, while value-creating strategies exploit opportunities provided by taking on risk. PRG extends to project programmes, defining the structure of project business cases, implementing a project value realisation methodology and developing a set of PRG performance metrics. The PMO is identified as the change agent for implementing PRG.

At the project level, project governance is distinguished from project management. Project risk perceptions are defined and evaluated and project risk appetite and tolerance are articulated. The contents of the project risk management plan is agreed and developed. There is an expectation that staff should be members of project management associations and gain certification. Desirable aspects of the soft PM paradigm are identified and implemented. Project risk management success factors are determined and monitored, and the design of a PRG maturity model commences.

LEVEL 4: MANAGED

Corporate governance recognises its important responsibility for risk management, and executive management engage with PRG. The organisation has changed from a hierarchical to an integrated PBO structure. Business and project strategies are aligned hierarchically, with project risk management part of the alignment. PRG processes and structures are implemented but differ for project portfolio, programmes and projects. Comprehensive business cases are developed by project sponsors and approved by steering committees. The latter fulfil 'broker' and 'steward' governance roles. Metrics measure and monitor PRG performance.

Project managers align project risk management with strategic goals and are conscious of the risk/reward equation. Projects adhere closely to the limits set for by the organisation's risk appetite and tolerance. The risk management plan is followed and regularly updated. A combination of qualitative and quantitative approaches is used to evaluate project risks. There is greater monitoring and control over project risk responses. Project members are rewarded for their professional memberships and certifications. Most project-based activities are managed in the soft project management paradigm. A model of PRG maturity is used to assess PRG performance.

LEVEL 5: OPTIMISED

At this level the organisation is project-based. Corporate governance principles aim to manage risk as a strategic dimension of business success. The board fully accepts overall responsibility for PRG and there is leadership capacity to support and shape PRG. Business and project strategies are integrated, with the proactive exploitation of positive project risk a strategic priority. Corporate, project and project risk governance activities overlap with a seamless integration of ERM and PRG. Implementation is effected through successful change management.

A comprehensive model of PRG exists and PRG processes are integrated across project portfolio, programmes and projects. Business cases include intangible project benefits and non-financial evaluations. Assurance is given that project benefits are realised as defined in the project business case. The PMO is regarded as the centre of excellence for project management and is the vehicle for integrating PRG structures and processes. Project risk appetite and tolerance are linked to the corporate governance style. The project risk register is the core repository for all information concerning the context in which project risk is managed. Most aspects of the soft paradigm have been adapted to PRG. The PRG maturity model is used to assess PRG sophistication.

Checklist: Implementation of Project Risk Governance Maturity Model

- Does the organisation use a PRG maturity model?

- Does the PRG maturity model assist in determining the organisation's level of PRG maturity?

- Does the PRG maturity model provide a roadmap for improving the performance of PRG?

- Should the PRG maturity model be modified to reflect new PRG approaches?

- Is PRG maturity regularly assessed?

Progressing Between Project Risk Governance Maturity Levels

The adoption of maturity models supports regular and systematic assessment of the organisation's capabilities. While theoretical frameworks provide the underlying conceptual understanding, the application of the model has to take place in the organisation's own context. The expectations of PRG performance are organisation-specific and the level of maturity to be achieved is determined according to its circumstances. The context in which a PRG maturity model is applied should take into account corporate and project strategy, resource constraints, criteria for project success, the ambitions and motivations of management, and so on. Furthermore, the assessment of PRG maturity should be based as much as possible on quantitative data rather than on feelings and opinions (Rad and Levin 2006).

Table 9.3 provides recommendations on strategies or activities that could be applied to move to the next level of PRG maturity. They are not exhaustive but intended to indicate the options that are available to an organisation. As such, they reflect the orientation to PRG of this book.

Table 9.3   Transition between project risk governance maturity levels

Transition	Key PRG Strategies and Activities
Level 1 (ad hoc) to Level 2 (initial) 'from negative to positive project risk management'	The board takes an interest in risk management. Focus on negative project risk with emerging focus on positive project risk. Recognition of importance of an ERM approach.
Level 2 (initial) to Level 3 (defined) 'development of formal PRG structures and relationships'	Project risk management included in project/ business strategy. Implementation of risk strategies for value-protecting. Implementation of risk strategies for value-creating. PRG processes, structures and relationships defined.
Level 3 (defined) to Level 4 (managed) 'enabling a predictable PRG approach'	Project risks are managed strategically. PMO is change agent for implementing PRG. Project manager aligns project risk management with strategic goals. Risk appetite and tolerance levels are clearly defined.
Level 4 (managed) to Level 5 (optimised) 'continuous improvement and embedded approach to PRG'	Move to an innovative and flexible PBO. Business/project/project risk strategy alignment is complete. Performance management criteria are applied. PRG maturity model assesses PRG sophistication.

There are number of factors that may impede the transition between stages.

- A lack of ready-to-use documentation. Models may exist in concept form and lack useful assessment guidelines for their application in practice. Models stimulate discussions within the organisation but not in sufficient depth because of the absence of documentation.

- The misapprehension that the higher the organisation is on the scale, the better. A case should be made for the level deemed appropriate for the organisation, based on the overall return on the investment of getting to the level. Vandersluis (2004) provided the example of the cost of implementing a culture change required to do Enterprise Project Management exceeding its potential benefits.

- The misapplication of the maturity model. There could be an error in the way the assessment was conducted because of inadequate supporting documentation. 'Determining the correct level of maturity in an organization is something less than a science and more than art' (Crawford 2006: 55). A potential disconnect could exist between conceptual design and actual organisational setting.

- The misuse of the maturity model to support the claim that there has been progress. As Crawford (2006) observed, organisations typically start with a baseline assessment which provides the basis to judge progress on a periodic basis.

To support movement along the stages of development, a number of prerequisites have to be satisfied (Crawford 2006; Pasian et al. 2012). First of all, project clients must be involved. The goals of the project must reflect customer interests, and hence the customer should be involved in defining them. They are stated at the beginning of the project and revisited throughout project implementation. This means that adaptable cultures must be fostered among staff to develop a willingness to accommodate new circumstances, methods or customer demands. There should be a recognition that there are aspects in organisational life that are inexact. However, an 'undefined' project raises questions and creates uncertainty. To generate the required trust, attitude and motivation, project goals should be clear and effectively communicated. To overcome any resistance to change, staff members should have an understanding of what the future holds for them. These prerequisites apply to both project and PRG maturity assessment.

Checklist: Progressing to the Next Level in the Project Risk Governance Maturity Model

- Are the differences between levels of PRG maturity clearly understood?

- Are strategies and activities developed to move to a higher level of PRG maturity?

- Is it understood that PRG maturity assessment can be misused?

- Is wide agreement obtained before attempting to move to the next level of PRG maturity?

- Is the move to another level of PRG maturity cost-effective?

Conclusion

This chapter introduced the nature of project management maturity models, before developing a model for PRG. The role of the model is to identify issues most critical to achieving PRG objectives according to dimensions and levels of maturity. Five levels were determined, ranging from an ad hoc to an optimised stage. Dimensions reflect the orientation to PRG by the author of this book. The model assists management to establish weaknesses in the current stage of reaching PRG maturity and serves as a roadmap for further improvement. The merit of the maturity model is to set direction, determine the actions required and encourage a culture change towards continuous improvement. Assessments are carried out periodically and provide a benchmark against which future progress or lack of it can be determined.

Appendix 1:
Survey of Key Issues in Project Risk Management

Introduction

Project risk management is a difficult task. First, complexity is brought about by uncertainty: we cannot accurately predict the future since this requires us to predict future opportunities and potential problems. Even our best attempts are not uniform, as various perspectives will exist. These surface when risks are identified and especially during risk analysis. Risk may be very clear to some but not to others and hence consensus is difficult to achieve. Furthermore, the process can be time consuming and its value and benefits are not always clear.

Research Study

The purpose of the research was to develop a list of project risk issues and make it available to project managers so that they could identify the most important issues from the list. To cover risks within the various activities of project management, reference to PMBOK® was made. According to PMBOK® (Project Management Institute 2008), project risk management can be defined as '[t]he systematic process of identifying, analyzing, and responding to project risk'. It is executed by completing the following steps: recognise the risk, investigate the risk, seek to deal with the risk, and keep track of the risk. They in turn are linked in PMBOK® with knowledge areas, as shown in Figure A1.1. PMBOK® also indicates the sequence in which a project risk is managed, namely Risk Management Planning → Risk Identification → Qualitative/Quantitative Risk Analysis → Risk Response Planning → Risk Monitoring and Control.

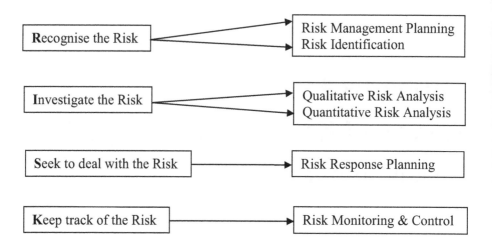

Figure A1.1   Outline of project risk management

The research material was developed in the form of 29 project risk issues that covered these activities from a review of the project risk management literature. Each risk issue was named and described, randomised and included in a questionnaire. The descriptions of the randomised 29 issues are shown in Table A1.2 at the end of this appendix.

Research participants were requested to rank each of the 29 risk issues according to their importance for the next three to five years. They were asked to consider how each issue may require special attention in the foreseeable future, which may be due to the increasing importance of the issue to the success of a project, not understanding the nature of the issue due to its complexity, continued difficulty in managing the issue, or changes expected in the nature of the issue. It was thought that, for the research to be useful, a forward-looking approach should be taken since, by gaining insight into risk issues that will confront them, project managers would be able to prepare themselves to effectively manage the key issues identified by the research.

First, a pilot study was conducted to reduce the 29 issues that had been identified to 10, to reach a greater consensus on the most important ones. This involved two groups: postgraduate students enrolled in the unit Project Risk Management, part of the Master of Project Management course at the author's university, and members of the AIPM. In the first group, 11 participants, mostly part-time students, completed a hard-copy questionnaire, while the second group participated in an online survey promoted and hosted by the Knowledge and Research Council of AIPM on its website. While 20 attempts were made to complete the online survey, only six completed the full questionnaire. Data from the two studies were combined to produce a ranking of the 29 issues.

Experiences gained from the pilot study provided the basis for designing the main study. It was clear from the pilot study that participants had found it difficult to rank 29 issues, as indicated by only six of the 20 online attempts being completed. Furthermore, research principles recommend that when using a forced ranking approach, the maximum number of issues should be 10. Following the suggestion of the AIPM, the researcher joined and presented the 10-issue survey to an online group of about 2,000 AIPM members using a LinkedIn forum. This enabled the researcher to encourage online discussions about the survey, thereby achieving greater participation and qualitative feedback on the risk issues presented.

Findings

Sixty-seven responses were received over a period of three months, December 2010 to February 2011. During the period, 11 comments were posted on the website by participants. This is feedback from a group of experienced project managers (half had 10–20 years of experience and one-third more than 20 years), who were mostly from the consulting/contracting field (56 per cent), with the majority rating their knowledge of project risk management as high.

Each issue was ranked according to the highest frequency it attracted for the ranking position. For example, for the issue 'Understanding the Risk Concept', 50 per cent of responses ranked the issue as number 1 while the next highest ranked issue for the number 1 position was 'Agreeing on what is Project Risk', ranked number 1 by 11.9 per cent of participants. For nine of the ranking position, an obvious issue could be identified; the exception was position number 8. This was allocated to the remaining issue, 'Developing Organisational Risk Processes'. In other words, the issue was not clearly the preferred number 8 ranking since this was 'Preparing the Risk Breakdown Structure' which, however, already occupied ranking position 6. This explains why the issue in second position at number 6 shows a higher frequency percentage in Table A1.1.

Table A1.1   Ranking of project risk issues

Rank	Issue	1st	2nd
1	Understanding the Risk Concept	50.0%	2 (11.9%)
2	Agreeing on what is Project Risk	28.4%	4 (16.9%)
3	Recognising Risk Events	23.4%	4 (15.4%)
4	Developing a Risk Management Approach	21.5%	7 (14.8%)
5	Preparing the Risk Management Plan	22.4%	7 (14.8%)
6	Preparing the Risk Breakdown Structure	18.2%	10 (15.6%)
7	Determining Risk Tolerance	18.0%	9 (14.7%)
8	Developing Organisational Risk Processes	10.6%	6 (16.7%)
9	Estimating Risk Severity	17.6%	10 (15.6%)
10	Creating and Updating the Risk Register	28.1%	6 (18.2%)

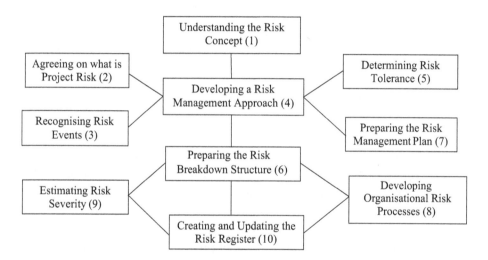

Figure A1.2   Perceived groupings and hierarchy of key project risk issues

From the results in Table A1.1, a certain pattern can be observed. For example, issue 4 is linked with issues 2 and 3 by being the second ranked issue for 2 and 3. At the same time, it is linked with issue 7 which is linked with issue 5. Issues 2, 3, 4, 5 and 7 can therefore be perceived as a grouping with issue 4 at its centre. This is shown in Figure A1.2, together with two further groupings derived from Table A1.1. Noticeably, issue 1 stands by itself at the top of the hierarchy.

Having identified the top 10 issues and grouped them according to their rankings, the following questions arose.

ARE WE ABLE TO IDENTIFY THE ISSUES GIVING RISE TO PROJECT RISK?

It was pointed out by participating practitioners that risk should not be perceived as a standalone concept but rather one that is determined by issues giving rise to risk. It is these issues that need to be identified and managed since, as observed by one participant, 'issues are linked to risk, in that if not appropriately managed, they can lead to risk moving from possibilities to certainties'.

CAN WE MANAGE THE COMPLEXITY OF PROJECT RISK?

Complexity arises since issues in projects are numerous, interrelated and involve a high degree of subjectivity in their evaluation. Issues need to be understood, their probabilities and consequences need to be assessed, and decisions have to be made to reduce them to an acceptable level.

DO WE ACKNOWLEDGE POSITIVE PROJECT RISKS?

The risk/return equation is well known: the higher the risk the greater the potential return. Yet it appears as if effective risk management and positive risk are not well understood. One participant expressed the concern that 'academia and AIPM still think risk processes are the same as effective risk management and seem to focus 100% on threats'. The goal of project risk management should be to minimise potential negative risks while maximising potential positive risks.

IS THE LOGICAL APPROACH APPROPRIATE?

The approach to managing project risk is usually well laid out in professional standards, such as PMBOK®, in what appears to be a logical and pragmatic manner. A logical approach can be justified if we have recurrent events that have recurrent conditions and could therefore be predicted and lend themselves to planning and control. However, this is rarely the case in practice as projects differ. Participants commented on risk events being observed and closely connected across multiple project activities: 'understanding the connectedness of risk across the PM functions and the importance of issues is something that doesn't seem to be understood or practised too well in project planning and implementation'.

CAN WE FIND THE RIGHT BALANCE?

The circumstances of a project can affect the risk management process, such as time pressure to get the job done and not being able to consult widely.

One participant commented: 'Identifying risk in the first place – business, operational or project deliverables – is one issue. I sometimes observe this being done by individual project managers in isolation under time pressure to get the risk form ticked off.' By contrast, too many risk events may be identified: 'I just reviewed a risk/opportunity plan for a tunnel project last month and realised that the contractor has just considered too many risks, so the schedule was so conservative and fatty.' This may well lead to unsatisfactory practice. 'I still see a trend among project managers to consider risk contingency as a bucket of slush for the unforeseen issues rather than isolating and actively managing each risk.'

CAN WE AGREE ON PROJECT RISK EVENTS AND TOLERANCE?

The need to include diverse opinions was confirmed by one of the participants: 'This [risk management approach] is about stakeholder engagement in the risk process and considering whole of life outcomes and sustainability.' The need to achieve a balance between formal processes and structure and human behaviour is reflected in a further observation: 'in applying risk management through two concepts – firstly embedding it into formal and routine processes so that it becomes part of one's habits; and two making the process rewarding in terms of user friendly' (sic). An indication was provided that a rigid approach to risk management may no longer be appropriate in the age of social media: 'risk management should be rapidly moving away from the physical and static risk to emerging stakeholder focused risks (threats and opportunities) created by the ability of people to spread opinion and information at the speed of light to 100s through social media'.

HOW DO WE DETERMINE PROJECT RISK SEVERITY?

There exists a close link between determining risk tolerance (issue number 5) and risk severity (issue number 9). Basic risk preferences can be observed in the way people behave in actual circumstances, i.e. how they might assess risk severity. This diversity potentially poses problems to the risk manager not familiar with human nature. He or she may observe different manifestations to risk-taking (for example when assessing risk severity) with different project members and under different circumstances. Yet attitudes to risk and its severity are critical for the project, as observed by one participant: 'Risk management starts with understanding risk tolerance (assuming management are mature enough to realise risk is inevitable) and the move into optimising accepted risk exposure balanced against the reward for accepting the risk.'

HOW CENTRAL IS PROJECT RISK DOCUMENTATION?

Both the risk breakdown structure and risk register are central to the project in that they capture the essence of project risk. In the former, risk is broken down into categories, subcategories and risk issues. Being linked with the WBS helps to define risk at the lowest level because risk is associated with project tasks, activity duration and project constraints. In the risk register, risk attributes are defined progressively over the course of a project to indicate potential risk events and related information such as risk triggers and responses. Both these documents are core to every project and both contain many subjective elements in their compilation, as outlined in previous discussions.

Conclusions

The merit of the research lies in a number of areas. First, an expert sampling approach was taken, i.e. respondents were chosen because of their expertise in the phenomenon being studied. Thus, their opinions on risk issues have a high level of credibility. Second, by choosing a ranking approach, participants had to determine the importance of risk issues relative to one another, i.e. the relationship between issues is measured, thereby producing a list of risk issues in order of their importance. A limitation of the approach, however, is that it does not give a statistical measure of the interval between issues. Third, the forward-looking approach used in the study enables project managers to concentrate their attention on the risk issues found to be most critical in the foreseeable future.

The issues that attracted most attention were about the nature of project risk. Considering that the majority of respondents were employed as consultants and contractors, with projects typically lasting between six and 20 months, gaining an understanding of project risk issues becomes critical since there has to be agreement with the project client about the existence of project risk. Issues ranked below the top three reflect a mixture of those relating to planning (developing a risk management approach and plan), the organisation (determining risk tolerance and risk processes) and risk analysis (estimating risk severity, preparing the risk breakdown structure and risk register).

What is noticeable is that the nature of risk analysis (qualitative and quantitative), as well as risk monitoring and control, were not highly ranked.

It may be that because they continue throughout the project they did not attract specific attention. As one participant insightfully commented, 'I felt the linear mode of the survey just a little arbitrary in reflecting a clear view.' This indicates that even our best attempts to manage project risk are not uniform, as various perspectives will exist. These surface when risks are identified, and especially during risk analysis. Risk may be very clear to some but not to others and hence consensus is difficult to achieve.

The above conclusion permits suggestions to be made about the direction of future research into gaining greater understanding of the nature of project risk. Qualitative research is best suited for this since it provides the ability to ask insightful questions on 'how' and 'why' project risk is difficult to operationalise. In contrast to the quantitative approach, the selection of qualitative research samples would be non-random, purposeful and small since it is desirable to interview experienced project risk managers who have given their profession much thought. A semi-structured interview method would be most appropriate since it provides structure (to focus on the research construct) as well as the opportunity to ask participants in-depth questions about their understanding of project risk. Flexibility is allowed through additional probing questions designed to encourage participants to clarify their responses, an outcome that would not have been available in a purely structured interview. Participants would be encouraged to freely share their relevant experiences or ideas if these were not covered in the structured questions. Questions would be developed from the findings of this study and a further literature review.

Acknowledgement

This appendix is an extract, reproduced, with permission, from the following publication:

Fink, D. (2012) 'Effective Risk Management: Insights from Australian Project Managers', *Proceedings of the Academy of World Business, Marketing and Management Development Conference*, 5(1), Budapest, Hungary.

Table A1.2   Randomised issues in project risk management

Developing Organisational Risk Processes Organisational processes are required to determine levels of risk in a project. They are incorporated in policies and cover risk tolerance, terms and concepts, templates and methodologies and allocation of responsibilities for risk management.
Preparing the Risk Breakdown Structure (RBS) To manage risk, it is broken down into categories, subcategories and risk issues. The Work Breakdown Structure (WBS) helps to define risk at the lowest level because risk is associated with project tasks, activity duration, project constraints, etc.
Identifying Specific Risk Events Project risk is difficult to determine since it can take many forms and can have a positive or negative effect on the project. The process itself is a continuous and iterative process throughout the project life cycle.
Simulating Project Risk A project simulation uses a model that translates the uncertainties specified at a detailed level into their potential impact on objectives that are expressed at the level of the total project. Monte Carlo analysis is such an example and requires quantitative skills.
Considering Project Change Requests These are requests to change the project and hence can result in new risks or new impacts of risks previously identified. They need to be analysed and documented for any changes required in the risk register, risk response plan, or risk management plan.
Creating and Updating the Risk Register The risk register is a document, often in table form, that contains the results of various risk management processes. It is created at the start of the project and progressively updated with potential risk events and related information such as risk triggers and responses.
Conducting Qualitative Risk Analysis When the organisation finds it is unable to put specific numbers on values it can use scales instead of specific estimates of risk. Estimates, however, are subjectively determined and processed and data quality depends on the expertise of the risk analyst.
Developing a Risk Management Approach Project risk management can be approached from many perspectives. For example, the risk focus of a project can be on satisfying the client's requirements at any cost or maximising risk efficiency by taking a cost-benefit perspective.
Estimating Risk Probability For each project risk event the probability or likelihood that the event will occur has to be established. This requires in-depth expertise with the project and/or extensive experiences with similar projects and associated risk management.
Integrating Project Risk Project risk is integrated with the other project activities such as time and resource scheduling to ensure the successful completion of the project. This is complex and requires ongoing project monitoring, making adjustments to project activities as required, etc.
Preparing the Risk Management Plan The plan provides a model on how to conduct project risk management. There are many aspects to consider. What should the plan include? What methods and tools are to be used? Who is doing what and how often? How will risk be reported, monitored, tracked?
Understanding the Risk Concept Determining risk is not well understood as it requires the consideration of different factors that give rise to risk. Risk is about identifying vulnerability and assessing vulnerability according to its likelihood and consequence.
Estimating Risk Impact For each project risk event the impact or amount of pain or gain the risk event poses to the project has to be established. This requires in-depth expertise with the project and/or extensive experience with similar projects and associated risk management.

Table A1.2 Randomised issues in project risk management *continued*

Complying with the Project Scope Statement
Risk management contributes to the project by ensuring that it is completed within the agreed project scope, i.e. the deliverables of the project are produced, the work required to create those deliverables is completed within expected time and cost budget, etc.

Selecting the Project Risk Team
Successful project risk management depends on the performance of the project members operating a team. Dysfunction among the team can arise due to conflict, disagreement, lack of commitment, avoidance of accountability, etc.

Establishing Project Success and Failure
Determining and then measuring success for a project requires defining what is success and failure, agreement among stakeholders and ongoing measurement of success or failure during the life of the project.

Carrying out Sensitivity Analysis
This approach, also called a 'what if?' analysis, measures the sensitivity of project objectives to changes in one variable while holding all other variables constant. Sensitivity analysis determines which risks have the most potential impact on project objectives.

Managing Project Risk People
The effectiveness of the project risk team should be maintained by drawing on research from psychologists and management theorists into managing people at work and include motivation theories and the social aspects of project teams.

Agreeing on Project Risk
The risk of a project sometimes may be very clear to some but not to others and hence consensus is difficult to achieve. Furthermore, the process of assessing and managing risk can be complex, time consuming and its value and benefits are not always obvious.

Determining Risk Tolerance
Risk tolerance is the amount of satisfaction or pleasure received from a potential payoff. Utility rises at a decreasing rate for organisations that are risk-averse. The organisation needs to determine its risk tolerance ranging from risk-seeking to being risk-averse.

Distinguishing Types of Risk
The concept of risk is usually related to an uncertain event or condition which, if it occurs, has a negative effect on the project objective. However, it is less understood that risk can have a positive effect on the project outcome, termed a positive risk.

Defining the Project
A project is a temporary endeavour undertaken to produce a unique product or service. It is difficult, however, to precisely determine either a definitive beginning and end or project uniqueness because every project is a new undertaking, often covering unfamiliar ground.

Auditing the Project
The project auditor is another project manager since he/she independently gathers information and documents about the project as it progresses. The focus of audit is on project effectiveness and efficiency, including project risk management.

Monitoring and Controlling Project Risk
Risk monitoring and control is a continuous, iterative process and, if done right, the project risk should 'never' occur. Responsibility has to be allocated for identifying risk triggers, responding to risk events and constantly evaluating existing and new project risk.

Assessing Risk Data Quality
Risk data is used to estimate risk probability and impact and requires accuracy, reliability and integrity of risk data. This can be assessed quantitatively (e.g. reliance on past data) or qualitatively (e.g. consulting experts).

Examining Environmental Factors
Project risk arises from the environment in which the project is completed. This is becoming increasingly complex, as has the impact on project risk. An approach used to examine the environment is a SWOT analysis.

Table A1.2   Randomised issues in project risk management *concluded*

Identifying Lessons Learned Lessons learned enable the organisation to improve its project management, including risk management, performance during subsequent projects. Experiences of the project team are established and recorded, and recommendations are made for future projects.
Responding to Project Risk Fundamental project risk response techniques/strategies include avoidance (eliminate risk), transference (pawn it off), mitigation (reduce its probability or impact) and acceptance (do nothing). The cost of response should not exceed its benefit.
Conducting Quantitative Risk Analysis This analysis focuses on numbers and uses numerical and/or statistical analysis. It is often preceded by qualitative risk analysis to identify the highest risks and risk thresholds, which are then subjected to the quantitative risk analysis approach.

Appendix 2:
Constructing a Business Case for Project Investments

The construction of a business case is part of the investment management process of PRG outlined in Chapter 4. Its key purpose is to develop an argument that convinces senior management to go ahead with the project investment. The case is expressed in business terms rather than technical terms to provide executive management with a clear indication of the attractiveness of the proposition. The business case is constructed, usually by the project sponsor, and presented for consideration to the steering committee for acceptance or rejection into the project portfolio.

It is worth reflecting on the definition of the nature of a business case provided by Remenyi and Remenyi (2009: 10).

> A business case is a justification for pursuing a course of action in an organisational context to meet the stated organisational objectives or goals. A business case frequently involves assessing the value of an investment in terms of its potential benefits and the resources required to set it up and to sustain it, i.e. its on-going costs. One of the major difficulties in producing a business case is the fact that benefits of an investment are often a function of the values of the organisation and the executives who are making the investment decisions. Thus a business case will inevitably have a significant degree of subjectivity associated with it.

Approach to Developing a Business Case

The business case should address the following topics.

PROJECT OBJECTIVES

When developing the business case, four key questions should be answered (ITGI 2006 – they are referred to as the four 'Ares'):

- Are we doing the right things? (the strategic questions).

- Are we doing them the right way? (the architecture questions).

- Are we getting them done well? (the delivery questions).

- Are we getting the benefits? (the value questions).

The strategic question is most important because it provides the answer to 'why' the project should be undertaken. It should demonstrate that the project will contribute to the strategic objectives of the organisation. The architecture question develops and evaluates options for satisfying the strategic objectives by addressing 'what' are the alternatives and 'which' one is the best. 'How' the project is executed supports the delivery question. The value question confirms that benefits are being obtained by completing a financial and/or non-financial analysis of estimated costs and benefits.

PROJECT COSTS AND BENEFITS

A key part of creating a business case is identifying potential benefits and identifying the costs required to generate those benefits. Not only do they have to be identified but also quantified, preferably in financial terms or otherwise in some other numeric form. They are only estimates because they are expectations of future events. For this reason, best-case/worst-case scenarios are developed to indicate the range of possibilities and probabilities. Data needs to be collected empirically from internal and/or external sources and validated through plausibility checks. Estimates are developed and 'owned' by the project sponsor and his/her team.

Project costs are generally easier to estimate than benefits. They are categorised as one-time or initial costs to cover expenses that are incurred at the start of the project. This could be the acquisition of equipment, such as computers, and setting up accommodation for the project team. From then on, ongoing expenditures are incurred such as the maintenance of computing systems, rent payments for accommodation, materials used and, of course, team members' remuneration. Project costs are also incurred to respond to identified project risks.

It is generally accepted that benefits flowing from an investment in projects are becoming harder to quantify in financial terms. The following examples illustrate this conundrum. Easily quantifiable project benefits can be readily expressed in monetary figures, such as staff savings following the introduction of a computerised system. Benefits that are not easily expressed in this way can, nevertheless, be operationalised in some number. For example, improved customer satisfaction can be measured on a rating scale, before the start and after the completion of the project. An improvement in the satisfaction rating would indicate a positive outcome for the project. Unquantifiable benefits are those that are regarded as intangible, such as the improvement in staff attitudes. They can be observed but are difficult to measure.

EVALUATION APPROACH

The expected costs and benefits are subjected to either a financial or non-financial analysis, or a combination. With financial analysis, the preference is for techniques that have been used over many years and are familiar to senior management. They are applied as a 'hurdle rate' to indicate the minimum outcome deemed necessary for the project to be considered for approval.

- Return on Investment (ROI). This is the annual benefit flowing from the investment divided by the total investment amount. It measures a simple rate of return expressed as a percentage. As such it is widely understood and used in business, particularly for new projects since the estimated ROI for competing project proposals can be compared and used to direct resources to those with the highest potential returns.

- Discounted Cash Flow (DCF). The cash flows from the investment and their timings over the project life are 'discounted' back to the start of the project using a risk-based discount rate. The rate indicates the level of uncertainty attached to outcomes that will materialise sometime in the future. In other words, future project returns are valued lower than returns that can be earned immediately.

- Net Present Value (NPV). Using the DCF estimates, a comparison is made between the discounted cash inflows and outflows, their net present values. A positive NPV means that inflows exceed outflows.

- Internal Rate of Return (IRR). This is the rate of return which causes the NPV to be zero. It is also referred to as the discounted cash flow return because it is the discount rate at which the net present value of costs (negative cash flows) of the investment equals the net present value of the benefits (positive cash flows) of the investment. From a financial perspective the organisation should undertake all projects with IRRs that exceed its cost of capital.

- Payback Period (PP). This divides the total investment by average annual net benefit to establish how long it takes to recoup the investment. It is widely used as a hurdle rate, i.e. a proposal will not be considered unless it falls below the nominated payback period. It is regarded particularly useful for a small project to demonstrate its obvious value, i.e. a very short payoff is equivalent to a high ROI.

The inclusion of a non-financial approach in the business case serves two purposes. It supports or even replaces the financial approach and provides additional information to the decision-making. As such it can support the financial analyses by 'strengthening' the numbers that have been calculated by providing positive supplementary information. The decision-maker will gain a better understanding of the overall strength of the proposed project because of the information that is provided.

There are essentially three types of non-financial approach to project appraisal: multi-criteria, strategic and portfolio (Harris et al. 2008). As the name applies, the multi-criteria approach combines various scores to provide multiple dimensions of project value. There are numerous dimensions that could be considered; Moutinho and Mouta (2011) claim that they could number as high as 400 for project evaluations. They arise from a wide range of sources including technical (e.g. to support innovation), commercial (e.g. to seize opportunities), political (e.g. to support environmental policies) and social (e.g. to improve the quality of life). They reflect the diversity of behavioural and organisational factors.

The strategic approach evaluates the project in the context of business goals. An example is the Balanced Scorecard (BSC) method. It measures the strategic values in four layers: financial, customer, business process and learning. Each layer has specific organisation-wide strategic objectives with defined metrics. The business case indicates how the strategic objectives will be met by meeting the expectations set out in the metrics.

Under the portfolio management approach, project investments are valued according to their contribution to a set of projects. This is akin to project programme management in which projects within the programme are related through sharing a common objective, client and/or resources, as well as through their interdependencies. The project programme achieves objectives or benefits that a single project alone cannot.

PROJECT RISK

Project risks play a critical role in the project achieving its objective, and their impact has to be clearly identified and included in the business case. They are identified, analysed and linked with response strategies and methods. Responses depend on the nature of the project risk, viz. being negative or positive. A range of response strategies (e.g. mitigate the impact of a negative risk) and associated response methods (e.g. mitigate the risks by imposing a control) have to be evaluated and costed. The cost of the risk response is included in the project evaluation approach that seeks to balance project costs with benefits.

Three types of risk should be identified in the business case: strategic, delivery and financial/non-financial. Strategic risks are linked to the likelihood of achieving project objectives. An example is managing project risk for organisational value-protecting and/or value-creating. Organisations are more familiar with the former since protecting assets through risk avoidance or reduction has been the traditional focus of risk management. With risk management taking on a proactive dimension, value-creating strategies are developed but there is less experience in their implementation.

Delivery risk is also referred to as risk associated with failure of execution and can be attributed to the novelty of the project and its size. The less familiarity there is among the project team with the nature of the project, and the larger its scope and the longer its duration, the greater is the risk of completing the project late or not at all. Some refer to the use of unproven technology by the project not as operating at the 'leading edge' but at the 'bleeding edge' in this respect.

Financial and non-financial risks are related to the accuracy with which project costs and benefits have been estimated. Tangible costs and benefits are generally easier to identify and quantify financially than intangible ones. However, they are still predictions and depend on underlying assumptions and sources of information. Variations can be established between best- and worst-case estimates, but even they depend on the quality of the data used and the ability of the estimator to include all costs and benefits. It is for this reason that estimates are not made by the project team but by the project sponsor and his/her team.

CHANGE IMPACT

The impact of the project on the organisation and/or its environment should be considered and included in the case analysis. For some project situations it may be possible to quantify the cost/benefit of the change impact, while for others a descriptive narrative becomes part of the business case. An example is the impact of the project on stakeholders and internal processes. Should the change be significant, a change management approach may be required and associated change management costs estimated and included in project costing.

RECOMMENDATIONS AND ACTION PLAN

One of the business case objectives is to address the 'architecture' question by developing and evaluating options about 'what' are the alternatives and 'which' one is the best. Each project has alternatives, even it is the most obvious one of 'doing nothing'. They provide the decision-makers with choices since they are not obliged to accept the one that is recommended in the business case report.

Each alternative is evaluated according to the same approach as outlined above. This provides a consistent framework for determining the merit of each option and for reaching a conclusion on an outcome that can be recommended to the decision-maker. While the core of the approach remains the same across all projects, variations may be introduced to take into consideration the uniqueness of individual projects and their contexts. The recommended (preferred) option is derived from the business case analysis. There needs to be a clear link between the two to justify the choice made. In other words, the recommendations flow logically from the completed analysis.

The recommendation is supported by an action plan. This addresses the decision-maker's question of 'what happens next?' Should the recommendation be accepted, a roadmap is provided on how to implement it. This would be straightforward if the recommendation were accepted as a whole, but becomes a matter of further discussion should only parts of the recommendation be accepted. Usually there is not a single recommendation but a number of primary ones supported by secondary ones to reflect the complexity of the business case outcomes.

OTHER COMPONENTS

Further material is provided in appendices. Among the more important ones are the assumptions underpinning the rationale of the business case. They include acknowledgment of the necessary conditions over which organisation has little or no control: risk events/conditions and constraints regarding costs and benefits. Detailed working sheets show how risks, costs and benefits were determined.

Criteria for the Business Case Report

A compelling business case has to be articulated and presented to the steering committee for approval. The following criteria should be addressed to ensure that the case is given serious consideration:

- The report has a definitive structure as set out in the next section. In other words, it follows a structure traditionally found in business reports such as background information, executive summary, analysis, and so on.

- The main purpose of a business report is to outline how project objectives will be met. An analysis is completed from which recommendations are derived. The analysis and recommendations are presented to management in a manner it can understand and evaluate.

- The merit of a business report is judged by management. They have to be satisfied with the analysis that was carried out so that they can decide with confidence whether or not to accept the recommendations of the report. They have the option to accept all, some or none of the recommendations.

- A business report is written in a language that reflects the professionalism and business knowledge of the writer. It should be addressed to senior management and adhere to a formal approach. It should avoid technical jargon that is not familiar to the readers of the report.

The Structure of a Business Case Report

The format of a business report can vary, but essentially it has the following structure:

- Cover. Title of report, to whom it is addressed, who has written it, date.

- Background information. A brief overview of the situation provides the rationale for the report. It provides information about the origins of the project and its context, and the terms of reference for the business case and how it was conducted.

- Executive summary. This summarises the total report. It is not background information or an introduction. By reading this summary, the reader is given an overview of how the analysis was done (approach), what was covered (scope), what were the main findings and recommendations, and what were the limitations of the report. The executive summary should appear early in the report because it is the section that will be read first.

- Analysis of the investment. This demonstrates the skill and knowledge of the analyst in evaluating the potential of the project. They should demonstrate both technical (project) and business (organisational) skills. The analysis is shown in two sections: in the body of the report to describe how the analysis was carried out and the analysis itself, and in appendices to provide worksheets containing details of facts and figures.

- Recommendations. These are derived from the analysis that was completed and therefore there has to be a logical connection between analysis and recommendations. Usually there are two or three primary recommendations and a number of secondary recommendations that support each of the primary recommendations.

- Limitations. This section covers the shortcomings of the analysis, for example that the report relied on the cost information provided by vendors. It is not about the limitations of the project itself but the report.

- Appendix. This includes detailed material such as worksheets and diagrams which were used to develop the analysis of the case. Because the business report should be in narrative form to make it readable to management, detailed workings are best placed in an appendix.

Figure A2.1 visualises the construction of the business case report. Following the professionally prepared cover, the background information section 'sets the scene' for the report. Similarly, the executive summary covers the content of the complete report as it is a 'summary' by definition. The analysis is the core of the report to which are linked the estimates of costs and benefits, and the impacts of risks and change. The evaluation considers alternatives, including the option of not doing anything. Recommendations flow from the evaluation, and limitations acknowledge the shortcomings of the completed business case.

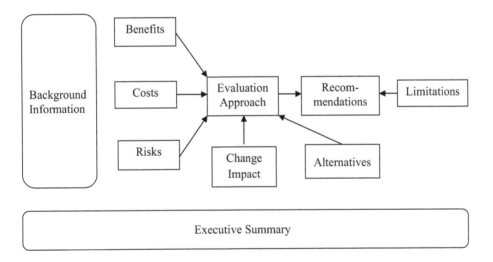

Figure A2.1   Visualising the business case report

Appendix 3:
A Project Risk Governance Maturity Model

Table A3.1 Levels and dimensions of a project risk governance maturity model

Projects in Organisations	Ad Hoc	Initial	Defined	Managed	Optimised
Project- versus Product-Based Organisation	Organisation is product-based with few projects	Increasing project activity	Project activities become formalised	Projects are managed professionally	Organisation is project-based
Project-Based Organisation (PBO) Characteristics	No or little awareness of a PBO	Some recognition of PBO advantages	PBO advantages and disadvantages are evaluated	PBO complexities recognised and managed	Comprehensive understanding of operating as a PBO
Project-Based Organisation Structure	PBO does not exist	Some features of a PBO are observed	PBO operates as a pyramid structure	Transition to an intergrated structure	An integrated organisational PBO structure
Business and Project Interaction	**Ad Hoc**	**Initial**	**Defined**	**Managed**	**Optimised**
Business Strategy Formulation	Business strategy is formulated superficially	Business strategy formulation is taken seriously	Formal processes exist for business strategy formulation	Business strategies are fully implemented	Effectiveness of business strategies is measured
Business and Project Strategy Alignment	Business strategy gives little consideration to projects	Business strategy begins to recognise importance of projects	Both business and project strategies are formulated	Business and project strategies are aligned hierarchically	Business and project strategies are integrated
Alignment with Project Risk Management	Project risk management not part of business strategy	Impact of project risks on business strategy is recognised	Project risk management included in project strategy	Project risk management part of business/project strategy alignment	Project risks recognised as adding strategic business value
Strategies for Value-Protecting	Emphasis is on identifying and managing negative project risks	Strategies emerge on how best to manage negative project risks	Value-protecting strategies developed for preventable and external project risks	Implementation of value-protecting strategies monitored	Support for value-protection permeates the organisation
Strategies for Value-Creating	Positive project risks are not or only superficially recognised	Obvious opportunities from positive project risks are recognised	Obvious value-creating strategies are developed and implemented	Full range of value-creating strategies are developed and implemented	Proactive exploitation of positive project risk is a strategic priority
Corporate and Project Governance	**Ad Hoc**	**Initial**	**Defined**	**Managed**	**Optimised**
Corporate Governance (CG)	CG practised in isolation	CG principles adapted to the organisation's characteristics	CG principles fully developed and published	CG principles recognise responsibility for risk management	CG principles manage risk as a strategic dimension of business success

	Ad Hoc	Initial	Defined	Managed	Optimised
Conformance and Performance	CG emphasises conformance aspects	Some recognition given to CG performance aspects	Both conformance and performance aspects of CG are defined	Conformance and performance aspects of CG are related to risk management	CG performance regularly reviewed and improved
Project Governance (PG)	No or little recognition of PG	Some recognition of the role of PG	PG is distinguished from project management	A behaviour-oriented view of PG	An outcome-oriented view of PG
Introduction to Project Risk Governance (PRG)	No or little recognition of PRG	Importance of PRG within PG starting to be recognised	Principles of PG and PRG are developed and articulated	PG and PRG are managed as separate responsibilities	CG, PG and PRG activities overlap
Project Risk Governance – Processes	**Ad Hoc**	**Initial**	**Defined**	**Managed**	**Optimised**
Scope of Project Risk Governance (PRG)	No or little recognition of PRG	Some recognition of the strategic role of project risk	PRG processes and structures are defined	PRG processes and structures are implemented	An integrated model of PRG operates
Portfolio, Programme, Project Management (PPPM)	Project portfolio is managed	Overall risk in project portfolio is assessed	PRG extends to project programmes	Role of PRG differs for PPPM	PRG processes are integrated across PPPM
Investment Management	Obvious project costs and benefits are recognised in project investments	Impact of project risks considered in project investments	Structure of project business cases defined	Business cases formally assessed by steering committees	Business cases include intangible benefits and non-financial evaluations
Value Realisation	No or little monitoring of project value realisation	Monitoring of realisation of major project costs, benefits and risks	Project value realisation methodology defined and implemented	Performance in project value realisation monitored	Benefits are realised as defined in the project business cases
Performance Management	PRG, if exists, is superficially monitored for performance	Some measures of PRG performance developed and monitored	Full set of PRG performance metrics defined	Full set of PRG performance metrics implemented and monitored	PRG performance metrics integrated with corporate performance metrics
Project Risk Governance – Structures and Relationships	**Ad Hoc**	**Initial**	**Defined**	**Managed**	**Optimised**
Organisational Leadership	No or little awareness of project risks among executives	Some recognition of the strategic importance of project risk	Executive management develops principles of PRG	Executive management take responsibility for PRG	Leadership capacity supports and shapes PRG
Board of Directors	Hands-off attitude by board to risk matters	Board focuses on Enterprise Risk Management (ERM)	Board demands attention given to PRG	PRG delegated to executive management	Board accepts overall responsibility for PRG

Table A3.1 Levels and dimensions of a project risk governance maturity model *continued*

	Ad Hoc	Initial	Defined	Managed	Optimised
Project Sponsors	Project sponsors focus solely on their relationship with project managers	Project sponsors link project investments to the project portfolio	Project sponsors prepare business cases for steering committees	Project sponsors responsible for success of project investments	Project sponsors focus on project investments in strategic areas
Project Managers	Project managers control the activities of projects	Project managers focus attention on project risk management	Project managers interact with project sponsors on strategic project risks	Project managers align project risk management with strategic goals	Project managers 'facilitate' project risk management
Steering Committees	Steering committees provide some control over project activities	Steering committees provide high-level control over project risk activities	Steering committees co-ordinate links between PRG structures	Steering committees fulfil 'broker' and 'steward' governance roles	Steering committees oversee performance of PRG
Project Management Office (PMO)	PMO focus only on project activities	PMO evolves organically to consider organisational issues	The role of PMO becomes that of a change agent	PMO is involved in implementing PRG	PMO is regarded as the centre of excellence for project management
Linking Structures and Processes	PRG structures and processes, if they exist, operate independently	It is accepted that PRG structures and processes require integration	Options to integrate PRG structures and processes are evaluated	PRG structures and processes are managed through the project life cycle	PRG structures and processes are linked through the PMO
Project Risk Governance in Context	**Ad Hoc**	**Initial**	**Defined**	**Managed**	**Optimised**
Professional Associations (PAs)	Some project team members belong to PAs	Project team members are encouraged to join PAs	Expectations for memberships and certifications are defined	Memberships and certifications are rewarded	Certifications reflect competence in project risk management
Risk Management Standards	No for few formal standards exist for ERM	Risk management standards provide a guide for ERM	ERM contributes to defining scope of PRG	ERM and PRG are managed separately	ERM and PRG are seamlessly integrated
Project Success	Success factors are linked to project management performance	Success factors are linked to project and project management performance	Project risk management success factors are defined	Project risk management success is measured and monitored	PRG success is measured for its contribution to business value
Human Resources Management (HRM)	No or few separate HRM practices for projects	Some HRM practices developed for projects	Project HRM focus on team dynamics and knowledge sharing	Project HRM practices consider the impermanence of projects	HRM practices for PRG are developed and implemented
Change Management	Some recognition of organisational change management models	Application of change management models at the organisational level	Impact of project changes on project risk is determined	PRG considers impact of project changes on project risk	PRG implemented through successful change management

Paradigmatic Influences	Only aspects of the hard paradigm are followed	Awareness of some aspects of the soft paradigm	Desirable aspects of the soft paradigm identified	Most project-based activities managed within the soft paradigm	Most aspects of the soft paradigm adapted to PRG
The Concept of Project Risk	**Ad Hoc**	**Initial**	**Defined**	**Managed**	**Optimised**
What is Project Risk? – The Basics	Uncertainty of project outcomes is understood	Wide variety of project risk sources are identified	Project risks are defined on the uncertainty spectrum	Information is collected about project risk uncertainty	Scope of project risk management covers full spectrum of uncertainty
Project Risk – A Deeper Perspective	Risk is not a phenomenon	Risk is socially constructed	Distinction between positive and negative project risks	The risk/reward equation is actively managed	Project risks are linked to business returns
Perceptions of Project Risk	Risk is not value-free	Different risk perceptions are recognised	Risk perceptions are defined and evaluated	Suitable project risk perceptions are adopted	Project risk efficiency strategies are implemented
Project Risk and Uncertainty	Concept of risk probability is known	Concepts of uncertainty and risk are differentiated	Characteristics of project risk events are defined	Limitations of probability-based approach are known	Own perceptions of project uncertainty and risk are developed
Project Risk Appetite and Tolerance	Project risk appetite and tolerance are inadequately defined	Importance of project risk appetite and tolerance is understood	Project risk appetite and tolerance are defined	Projects adhere to project risk appetite and tolerance limits	Project risk appetite and tolerance fit corporate governance style
Essentials of Project Risk Management	**Ad Hoc**	**Initial**	**Defined**	**Managed**	**Optimised**
Understanding Projects	Key features of projects are recognised	Concept of project life cycle is understood	Project risks and rewards during life cycle are identified	Financial exposure during project life cycle is monitored	Projects deliver a net financial benefit to the organisation
Importance of Project Risk Management (PRM)	Immaturity of PRM as a knowledge area is not recognised	Importance of PRM as a PM knowledge area is understood	Strategies for PRM are evaluated and defined	Strategies for PRM are implemented	Attention is given to key issues research in PRM
Project Risk Management Plan (RMP)	No or little planning for the project RMP	Inputs to the project RMP are identified and collected	Contents of Project RMP are agreed and developed	Project RMP is followed and regularly updated	Project RMP is comprehensive and includes reporting requirements
Project Risk Modelling and Ranking	Distinction made between qualitative and quantitative approaches	Qualitative analysis used to evaluate project risk events	Quantitative analysis used to evaluate project risk events	Combination of qualitative and quantitative approaches used	Complexity of project risk ranking is taken into account in risk responses

Table A3.1   Levels and dimensions of a project risk governance maturity model *concluded*

	Ad Hoc	Initial	Defined	Managed	Optimised
Project Risk Register (PRR)	No or only a superficial PRR is maintained	The PRR is opened as a spreadsheet or table	PRR lists all identified risk events and conditions and their current status	Entries in PRR are used to track risk response implementation	PRR provides full contextual information for project risks
Implementing Project Risk Responses	Implementation of project risk responses is neglected	Management has concerns about project risk response implementation	Monitoring and control activities are designed	Active monitoring and control over project risk responses	Project risk responses are supplemented with a contingency plan
Project Team	No or little attention is given to the functioning of the project team	Factors that cause team dysfunction are identified and addressed	Desirable social styles and motivation factors are defined	Team members with suitable social and motivation factors are recruited	Social and motivation factors are known for each project member
Project Risk Governance Maturity	**Ad Hoc**	**Initial**	**Defined**	**Managed**	**Optimised**
Project Management Maturity Models	No or little use of project management maturity models	The merits of project management maturity models are explored	A suitable project management maturity model is identified	The selected project management maturity model is implemented	The features of project management maturity models are adapted to PRG
Benefits of Maturity Assessment	No or little awareness of assessing maturity	The benefits of assessing maturity are identified	Data is collected to establish level of maturity within the model	The maturity model provides a roadmap for improved performance	The organisation establishes its ideal position within the maturity model
Maturity Levels and Dimensions	No or little awareness of maturity levels and dimensions	Maturity levels and dimensions in existing models are examined	Maturity levels and dimensions suitable for the organisation are defined	Maturity levels and dimensions are implemented in a maturity model	The effectiveness of maturity levels and dimensions is regularly reviewed
A PRG Maturity Model	No or little awareness of a PRG maturity model	Levels/dimensions for a PRG maturity model are developed	A model of PRG maturity model is defined	The model of PRG maturity is implemented	The PRG maturity model links project and business strategy
Progressing between PRG Maturity Levels	No or little guidance on transiting between maturity levels	Broad transition goals are established	Documentation guides transition between maturity levels	Transition between maturity levels is part of change management	The implications of assessing PRG maturity are acknowledged

References

Abu Hassim, A., Kajewski, S. and Trigunarsyah, B. (2011), 'The Importance of Project Governance Framework in Project Procurement Planning', *Procedia Engineering*, 14, 1929–37.

Alavi, M. and Leidner, D.E. (2001), 'Knowledge Management and Knowledge Management Systems: Conceptual Foundations and Research Issues', *MIS Quarterly*, 25(1), 107–36.

Aubry, M., Hobbs, B. and Thuillier, D. (2007), 'A New Framework for Understanding Organisational Project Management Through the PMO', *International Journal of Project Management*, 25, 328–36.

Aubry, M., Muller, R., Hobbs, B. and Blomquist, T. (2010), 'Project Management Offices in Transition', *International Journal of Project Management*, 28, 766–78.

Australian Stock Exchange Corporate Governance Council (2010), *Corporate Governance Principles and Recommendations with 2010 Amendments*, 2nd edition, Sydney: ASX Corporate Governance Council.

Barkley, B.T. (2004), *Project Risk Management*, New York: McGraw-Hill.

Belev, G.C. (1989), 'Minimizing Risk in High Technology Programs', *Cost Engineering*, 31(10), 11–14.

Besner, C. and Hobbs, B. (2012), 'The Paradox of Risk Management: A Project Management Practice Perspective', *International Journal of Managing Projects in Business*, 5(2), 230–47.

Bredillett, C.N. (2008), 'Exploring Research in Project Management: Nine Schools of Project Management Research (Part 4)', *Project Management Journal*, March, 2–6.

Bredillett, C.N., Ruiz, P. and Yatim, F. (2008), 'Investigating the Development of Project Management: A Time–Distance Analysis Approach of G8, European G6, and Outreach 5 Countries', *Proceedings of PMI Research Conference*, Warsaw.

Burnaby, P. and Hass, S. (2009), 'The Steps to Enterprise-Wide Risk Management', *Corporate Governance*, 9(5), 539–50.

Chapman, C. (2006), 'Key Points of Contention in Framing Assumptions for Risk and Uncertainty Management', *International Journal of Project Management*, 24, 303–13.

Chapman, C. and Ward, S. (2003), *Project Risk Management*, West Sussex: John Wiley & Sons.

Chapman, C. and Ward, S. (2004), 'Why Risk Efficiency is a Key Aspect of Best Practice Projects', *International Journal of Project Management*, 22, 619–32.

Childress, D.R. (1962), 'Contributions to Risk and Insurance Theory from the Field of Philosophy', *Journal of Risk and Insurance*, 29(3), 321–8.

Cicmil, S., Williams, T., Thomas, J. and Hodgson, D. (2006), 'Rethinking Project Management: Researching the Actuality of Projects', *International Journal of Project Management*, 24, 675–86.

CIMA (2004), *Enterprise Governance – A CIMA Discussion Paper*, available at http://www.cimaglobal.com/Documents/importedDocuments/tech_dispap_enterprise_governance_2004.pdf [accessed 28 June 2013].

Cooke-Davies, T. (2002), 'The "Real" Success Factors of Projects', *International Journal of Project Management*, 20, 185–90.

Crawford, J.K. (2006), 'The Project Management Maturity Model', *Information Systems Management*, 23(4), 50–58.

Dali, A. and Lajtha, C. (2012), 'ISO 31000 Risk Management – "The Gold Standard"', *The EDP Audit, Control, and Security Newsletter*, 45(5), 1–8.

De Reyk, B., Grushka-Cockayne, Y., Lockett, M., Calderini, S.R., Moura, M. and Sloper, A. (2005), 'The Impact of Portfolio Management on Information Technology Projects', *International Journal of Project Management*, 23, 524–37.

Desouza, K.C. and Evaristo, J.R. (2006), 'Project Management Offices: A Case of Knowledge-Based Archetypes', *International Journal of Information Management*, 26, 414–23.

Du, L. and Shi, Y. (2007), 'Implement Business Strategy via Project Portfolio Management: A Model and Case Study', *Journal of American Academy of Business*, 11(2), 239–44.

Ernst & Young (2012), *Turning Risk into Results – How Leading Companies Use Risk Management to Fuel Better Performance*, available at http://www.ey.com/publication/vwluassets/turning_risk_into_results:_how_leading_companies_use_risk_management_to_fuel_better_performance/$file/ey%20turning%20risk%20into%20results%20final.pdf [accessed 28 June 2013].

Everett, C. (2011), 'A Risky Business: ISO 31000 and 27005 Unwrapped', *Computer Fraud & Security*, February, 5–7.

Fink, D. (2006), 'Value Decomposition for E-Commerce Performance', *Benchmarking: An International Journal*, 13(1/2), 81–92.

Fink, D. (2012), 'Project Risk Management: Insights from Australian Project Managers', *Proceedings of Academy of World Business, Marketing and Management Development Conference*, 5(1), Budapest.

Gareis, R. (2010), 'Changes of Organizations by Projects', *International Journal of Project Management*, 28, 314–27.

Garratt, B. (2007), 'Dilemmas, Uncertainty, Risks, and Board Performance', *BT Technology Journal*, 25(1), 11–18.

Hanstad, D.V. (2012), 'Risk Management in Major Sporting Events: A Participating National Olympic Team's Perspective', *Event Management*, 16, 189–201.

Harris, M.D.S., Herron, D. and Iwanicki, S. (2008), *The Business Value of IT*, London: Taylor & Francis Group.

Hartman, F. and Ashrafi, R. (2004), 'Development of the SMART Project Planning Framework', *International Journal of Project Management*, 22, 499–510.

Heitger, B. and Doujak, A. (2008), *Management Cuts and New Growth – An Innovative Approach to Change Management*, Vienna: Goldegg.

Heldman, K. (2005), *Project Manager's Spotlight on Risk Management*, San Francisco: Jossey-Bass.

Henderson, J.C., Venkatraman, N. and Oldach, S. (1996), 'Aligning Business and IT Strategies', in J.N. Luftman (ed.), *Competing in the Information Age: Strategic Alignment in Practice*, Oxford: Oxford University Press.

Hermanson, D.R. (2003), 'The Implications of COSO's Proposed ERM Framework', *Internal Auditing*, 18(6), 41–3.

Hopkinson, M. (2011), *The Project Risk Maturity Model Measuring and Improving Risk Management Capability*, Surrey: Gower Publishing.

Huemann, M., Keegan, A. and Turner, J.R. (2007), 'Human Resource Management in the Project-Oriented Company: A Review', *International Journal of Project Management*, 25, 315–23.

ISACA (2009), *The Risk IT Practitioner Guide*, available at http://www.isaca.org/Knowledge-Center/Research/ResearchDeliverables/Pages/The-Risk-IT-Practitioner-Guide.aspx [accessed 28 June 2013].

ITGI (2003), *Board Briefing on IT Governance*, 2nd edition, available at http://www.isaca.org/Knowledge-Center/Research/ResearchDeliverables/Pages/Board-Briefing-on-IT-Governance-2nd-Edition.aspx [accessed 28 June 2013].

ITGI (2006), *Enterprise Value: Governance of IT Investments: The Business Case*, available at http://www.isaca.org/Knowledge-Center/Val-IT-IT-Value-Deli very-/Documents/VAL-IT-business-case.pdf [accessed 28 June 2013].

Jaeger, J. (2012), *New COSO Guidance on Managing Risks from Cloud Computing*, available at http://www.complianceweek.com/new-coso-guidance-on-managing-risks-from-cloud-computing/article/249203/ [accessed 28 June 2013].

Kaplan, R.S. and Mikes, A. (2012), 'Managing Risks: A New Framework', *Harvard Business Review*, June, 49–60.

Kendrick, T. (2004), 'Strategic Risks: Am I Doing OK?', *Corporate Governance*, 4(4), 69–77.

Kerr, G. (2005), 'Reflections on "The Steering Committee"', *American Journal of Evaluation*, 26, 132–4.

Knight, F.H. (1921), *Risk, Uncertainty and Profit*, Boston: Houghton Mifflin.

Kotter, J. (1996), 'Successful Change and the Force that Drives It', *The Canadian Manager*, 21(3), 20–23.

Koulbanis, N. (2003), 'Total Value of Opportunity: Using Business Metrics to Shed Light on IT Investments', *Proceedings of Gartner Symposium*, Sydney.

Kutsch, E. and Hall, M. (2010), 'Deliberate Ignorance in Project Risk Management', *International Journal of Project Management*, 28, 245–55.

Kwak, Y.H. and Ibbs, C.W. (2002), 'Project Management Process Maturity (PM)^2 Model', *Journal of Management Engineering*, 18, 150–55.

Landaete, R.E. (2008), 'Evaluating Benefits and Challenges of Knowledge Transfer Across Projects', *Engineering Management Journal*, 20(1), 29–38.

Lechler, T.G. and Cohen, M. (2009), 'Exploring the Role of Steering Committees in Realizing Value from Project Management', *Project Management Journal*, March, 42–54.

Leitch, M. (2010), 'ISO 31000:2009 – The New International Standard on Risk Management', *Risk Analysis*, 30(6), 887–92.

Levy, A. and Merry, U. (1986), *Organizational Transformation – Approaches, Strategies and Theories*, New York: Greenwood Publishing Group.

Lewin, K. (1947), 'Frontiers in Group Dynamics', *Human Relations*, 1(1), 5–41.

Marnewick, C. and Labuschagne, L. (2011), 'An Investigation into the Governance of Information Technology Projects in South Africa', *International Journal of Project Management*, 29, 661–70.

McKeen, J.D. and Guimaraes, T. (1985), 'Selecting MIS Projects by Steering Committee', *Communications of the ACM*, 28(12), 1344–52.

Moody, M.J. (2004), 'COSO Framework on ERM is Half-Baked', *Rough Notes*, 147(4), 62–3.

Moody, M.J. (2010), 'ERM & ISO 31000', *Rough Notes*, 153(3), 80–81.

Morris, P.W.G., Crawford, L., Hodgson, D., Shepherd, M.M. and Thomas, J. (2006), 'Exploring the Role of Formal Bodies of Knowledge in Defining a Profession – The Case of Project Management', *International Journal of Project Management*, 24, 710–21.

Morris, P.W.G. (2009), 'Research and the Future of Project Management', *International Journal of Managing Projects in Business*, 3(1), 139–46.

Moutinho, N. and Mouta, H. (2011), 'Project Appraisal: A Reflection', *Proceedings of 2nd International Conference on Construction and Project Management*, Singapore.

Mueller, R. (2009), *Project Governance*, Farnham: Gower Publishing.

Mueller, R. and Jugdev, K. (2012), 'Critical Success Factors in Projects: Pinto, Slevin, and Prescott – The Elucidation of Project Success', *International Journal of Managing Projects in Business*, 5(4), 757–75.

Munns, A.K. and Bjeirmi, B.F. (1996), 'The Role of Project Management in Achieving Project Success', *International Journal of Project Management*, 14(2), 81–7.

Nonaka, I. and Takeuchi, H. (1995), *The Knowledge Creating Company: How Japanese Companies Create the Dynamics of Innovation*, Oxford: Oxford University Press.

OECD (2004), *OECD Principles of Corporate Governance*, Paris: OECD Publications Services.

Outperform (2012), *Capability Maturity Models – Using P3M3 to Improve Performance*, available at http://www.vanharen-library.net/Documents/capability_maturity_models_-_using_p3m3_to_improve_performance.pdf [accessed 28 June 2013].

Oxford Dictionaries (n.d.), available at http://oxforddictionaries.com/definition/english/govern [accessed 28 June 2013].

Pasian, B., Sankaran, S. and Boydell, S. (2012), 'Project Management Maturity: A Critical Analysis of Existing and Emerged Factors', *Internal Journal of Managing Projects in Business*, 5(1), 146–57.

Pearce, J.A. and Robinson, R.B. (1997), *Formulation and Control of Competitive Strategy*, Boston: Irwin.

Peltokorpi, V. and Tsuyuki, E. (2006), 'Knowledge Governance in a Japanese Project-Based Organization', *Knowledge Management Research & Practice*, 4, 36–45.

Pender, S. (2001), 'Managing Incomplete Knowledge: Why Risk Management Is Not Sufficient', *International Journal of Project Management*, 19, 79–87.

Peterson, R.R. (2003), 'Information Strategies and Tactics for Information Technology Governance', in W. van Grembergen (ed.), *Strategies for Information Technology Governance*, London: Idea Group.

Pollack, J. (2007), 'The Changing Paradigms of Project Management', *International Journal of Project Management*, 25, 266–74.

Porter, M. (1980), *Competitive Advantage*, New York: Free Press.

Project Management Institute (2008), *A Guide to the Project Management Body of Knowledge*, Pennsylvania: SAI Global.

Project Manager (2012), 'Top Trends to Watch', February 9, 8–9.

Rad, P.F. and Levin, G. (2006), 'Project Management Maturity Assessment', *AACE International Transactions*, PM.06, 1–4.

Regev, S., Shtub, A. and Ben-Haim, Y. (2006), 'Managing Project Risks as Knowledge Gaps', *Project Management Journal*, 37(5), 17–25.

Remenyi, D., Bannister, F. and Money, A. (1997), *Achieving Maximum Value from Information Systems: A Process Approach*, West Sussex: John Wiley & Sons.

Remenyi, D. and Remenyi, B. (2009), *How to Prepare Business Cases*, Oxford: CIMA Publishing.

Renn, O. (2010), *Risk Governance: Coping with Uncertainty in a Complex World*, London: Earthscan.

Sanchez, H., Robert, B., Bourgault, M. and Pellerin, R. (2009), 'Risk Management Applied to Projects, Programs, and Portfolios', *International Journal of Managing Projects in Business*, 2(1), 14–35.

Schlichter, J., McEver, J. and Hayes, R.E. (2010), 'Maturity Frameworks for Enterprise Agility in the 21st Century', *Proceedings of PMI Global Congress*, North America.

Schoemaker, P.J.H. (1993), 'Determinants of Risk-Taking: Behavioral and Economic Views', *Journal of Risk and Uncertainty*, 6, 49–73.

Schwalbe, K. (2007), *Information Technology Project Management*, Canada: Thomson Learning.

Scott, A. (2004), 'COSO ERM Framework Released', *The Internal Auditor*, 61(5), 17–18.

Sewchurran, K., Smith, D. and Roode, D. (2010), 'Towards a Regional Ontology for Information Systems Project Management', *International Journal of Managing Projects in Business*, 3(4), 681–92.

Sharma, D., Stone, M. and Ekinci, Y. (2009), 'IT Governance and Project Management: A Qualitative Study', *Database Marketing & Customer Strategy Management*, 16(1), 29–50.

Stare, A. (2010), 'Comprehensive Management of Project Changes', *Economic and Business Review*, 12(3), 195–210.

Steinberg, R.M. (2011), *Using the New COSO Risk-Management Guidance*, available at http://www.complianceweek.com/using-the-new-coso-risk-man agement-guidance/article/195885/ [accessed 28 June 2013].

Taliento, M. (2007), 'The Role and the Ambit of Corporate Governance and Risk Control Frames', *The Journal of American Academy of Business*, 11(2), 251–6.

Thiry, M. and Deguire, M. (2007), 'Recent Developments in Project-Based Organisations', *International Journal of Project Management*, 25, 649–58.

Thompson, P.B. (2007), 'Norton's Sustainability: Some Comments on Risk and Sustainability', *Journal of Agriculture and Environmental Ethics*, 20, 375–86.

Trowler, P. (1997), 'Beyond the Robbins Trap: Reconceptualising Academic Response to Change in Higher Education (or Quiet Flows the Don?)', *Studies in Higher Education*, 22(3), 301–18.

Turner, J.R. and Keegan, A. (2001), 'Mechanisms of Governance in the Project-Based Organization: Roles of the Broker and Steward', *European Management Journal*, 19(3), 254–67.

Turner, J.R. and Mueller, R. (2003), 'On the Nature of the Project as a Temporary Organization', *International Journal of Project Management*, 21, 1–8.

UK Financial Reporting Council (2010), *The UK Corporate Governance Guide*, London: Financial Reporting Council.

Unger, B.N., Gemuden, H.G. and Aubry, M. (2012), 'The Three Roles of a Project Portfolio Management Office: Their Impact on Portfolio Management Execution and Success', *International Journal of Project Management*, 30, 608–20.

US Business Roundtable (2010), *Principles of Corporate Governance*, Washington: Business Roundtable.

Vandersluis, C. (2004), 'Five Degrees of Excellence with Project Management Maturity', *Computing Canada*, 30(6), 13.

Ward, S.C. (1999), 'Assessing and Managing Important Risks', *International Journal of Project Management*, 17(6), 331–6.

Weill, P. (2004), 'Don't Just Lead, Govern: How Top-Performing Firms Govern IT', *MIS Quarterly Executive*, 3(1), 1–17.

Wikipedia (2013), *OPM3*, available at http://en.wikipedia.org/wiki/OPM3 [accessed 28 June 2013].

Williams, T.M. (2005), 'Assessing and Moving On from the Dominant Project Management Discourse in the Light of Project Overruns', *IEEE Transactions on Engineering Management*, 52, 497–508.

Williams, T., Lakegg, O.J., Magnussen, O.M. and Glasspool, H. (2010), 'An Investigation of Governance Frameworks for Public Projects in Norway and the UK', *International Journal of Project Management*, 28, 40–50.

Winter, M., Smith, C., Morris, P. and Cicmil, S. (2006), 'Directions for Future Research in Project Management: The Main Findings of a UK Government-Funded Research Network', *International Journal of Project Management*, 24, 638–49.

Wyman, O. (2012), *Maximizing Returns on Large Investment Projects*, New York: Marsh & McLennan Companies.

Yeo, K.T. and Ren, Y. (2009), 'Risk Management Capability Maturity Model for Complex Product Systems (CoPS) Projects', *Systems Engineering*, 12(4), 275–94.

Young, R. and Jordan, E. (2008), 'Top Management Support: Mantra or Necessity?' *International Journal of Project Management*, 26, 713–25.

Young, R., Young, M., Jordan, E. and O'Connor, P. (2012), 'Is Strategy Being Implemented Through Projects? Contrary Evidence from a Leader in New Public Management', *International Journal of Project Management*, 30, 887–900.

Zimmerman, J.W. (2002), 'Is Your Company at Risk? Lessons from Enron®', *USA Today®*, 1, 27–9.

Index

For Product Safety Concerns and Information please contact our
EU representative GPSR@taylorandfrancis.com Taylor & Francis
Verlag GmbH, Kaufingerstraße 24, 80331 München, Germany